The Suburban Wild

The Suburban Wild

BY PETER FRIEDERICI

The University of Georgia Press

Athens and London

Published by the University of Georgia Press

Athens, Georgia 30602

© 1999 by Peter Friederici

All rights reserved

Designed by Sandra Strother Hudson

Set in Minion

Printed and bound by Maple-Vail

The paper in this book meets the guidelines for
permanence and durability of the Committee on
Production Guidelines for Book Longevity of the
Council on Library Resources.

Printed in the United States of America

03 02 01 00 99 C 5 4 3 2 1

Library of Congress Cataloging-in-Publication Data

The suburban wild / by Peter Friederici.

    p.   cm.

Includes bibliographical references.

ISBN 0-8203-2134-6 (alk. paper)

1. Nature. 2. Natural history. 3. Urban ecology (Biology)

I. Friederici, Peter, 1963– .

QH81.S8775 1999

508—DC21   99-25399

          CIP

British Library Cataloging-in-Publication Data available

"A Green Heron" was first published in *Trapeze,* spring 1996.
"Pigeons," an earlier version of "Mussels," and "Ducks" were first
published in the *Reader,* September 13, 1996; November 6, 1992;
and November 4, 1994. "Tracks" was first published in *Wild Earth,*
spring 1998.

FOR MY PARENTS

Contents

The Suburban Wild

This, too, was good to know.
Though much has been lost, much remains.
EDWARD ABBEY
One Life at a Time, Please

MARCH: *Geese*

We are flying in from the west. We pass through a darkness of clouds that abruptly loosens, suffuses pale salmon as if we were descending into dawn, and then tears apart to reveal the city, glowing in the winter evening. We're over the Loop, its skyscrapers reaching improbably high toward us, bejeweled with lights. The canyons in between are electric with cars.

We dip, swing, circle wide over the endless blackness that is the lake: nothing. Then back over the north side, where from this height one socioeconomic class blends almost imperceptibly into another, townhouses and three-flats and public housing projects all melded into one steadily luminescing patchwork of electricity. The perfect lines of streets head on into the suburbs, straight as desire; they glisten wet. Headlights and taillights parse out the city's pulse.

The plane descends further, into its final approach. Suddenly comes below a patch of unexplained nothing, a blankness, a lightless void. I strain my eyes: what is this place? Finally as we pass I can glean at its edge the glow of streetlights silhouetting leafless branches. It is a forest preserve, an island of trees, a rectilinear patch of woods hemmed in by roads and neighborhoods and boxy factory buildings. Cars glide by its wet edges.

We touch down smoothly on the rain-slicked runway. As we taxi through the lurid lights of the airport I am caught up in the emotions of revisiting the town I grew up in and seeing relatives again, but still that black square of forest stays with me, the tantalizing void that from above so resembled the unseen face of the lake.

Wherever I go I am drawn to such blank spaces, to white patches on the map: interstices, forgotten places defined by absence. I cannot stay away from the remnant woods and marshes and fields where the only light at night comes from the pale rosy glow of streetlights reflected back from the clouds. I seek out muddy margins and weedy places, empty spaces where winged seeds of aster and goldenrod hang clumped and sodden in the death of winter, where old vines of poison ivy set cord-thin snares across the gaps between trees. I meander to marshy edges where mud freezes black around the bases of slender cattail stalks. I linger in the leftovers that we have either neglected or set aside as luxuries—places to take an autumn weekend's walk, go sledding, make out, walk the dog, dump a body. I live in a house, drive a car, fly in planes, and work on a computer, but increasingly it seems to me that these wedges and blocks of undeveloped land lie near the core of my life.

Which is why I am out early the next morning, so thoroughly wrapped up in coat and hat and gloves and boots that I can barely bend my neck to look up into the trees. The calendar says March, but land and sky still appear locked in deepest winter. The wind has come straight from the Arctic. Above me I can hear its myriad creakings and rustlings and eerie groanings in the branches, the continuous restless scrapings of twigs one on another.

Awkwardly craning my neck, I search the treetops, my eyes drawn by the constant motion, hoping to spot chickadees, woodpeckers, nuthatches, the few but lively birds of winter. But each time I am fooled anew by twigs and branches; no birds fly or hop or peer for food in crevices of wood. Wiser than I, they have all gone to thicker woods, backyard feeders, the shelter of shrubs. There are no birds to watch and so for want of anything better to do I find myself reading the elaborate calligraphy that winter trees draw on the soft-bellied pages of sky, day after overcast day. Each tree writes its own life story, from the thickness of the trunk thrusting up from hard-frozen soil to the gap where a branch shattered in a thunderstorm last summer to the last and most delicate filigrees of twigs scraping their first winter's tales against one another as the cold winds blow.

Every tree has its own distinctive script. The branches and twigs of the ashes fork in perfect symmetry, reaching almost straight toward the sky, each junction repeating the exact same acute angle of every other one. There are no right angles in a leafless ash tree. An ash is the perfect splayed diagram of an ideal family tree, each child producing two more children. It is the Euclidean ideal of treeness.

The few shagbark hickories that grow among the oaks bear odd protuberances near the ends of their bare twigs, as if a clumsy artist in drawing them let the pen linger too long at the end of each stroke, leaving a blot of ink as black as the crows whose quick-winged flights overhead seem the only sign of animal life in the dull bleakness of air and land.

The oaks have the most individual character, their branches reaching out thick and horizontal as if in defiance of wind and gravity. The trunks of bur oaks are stout, cylindrical. Their branches remain thick almost to their ends, where they sprout in a final flurry of small twigs. The effect is ungainly: it looks to me as if they were growing upside down, a thick taproot reaching high into the air while the branches—which surely must be more graceful—burrow by mistake into the ground. The white oaks, with branches almost as thick and convoluted, still bear a few lingering red-brown leaves, ragged and rustling. It's a small comfort, this sign that summer once passed this way, and without it we might lose all hope that warm weather might ever come again—as is not so hard to do on a grainy and monochromatic March day, with the frigid wind blowing once again, the sidewalks iced over, again, and no sign of the sun, as usual.

At the midpoint of my walk, by the railroad tracks, two huge willows sport extravagant showers of tawny drooping twigs, almost yellow, that in their rowdy abundance and bright color seem an affront to the somber spirit of winter, a reckless claim to life and color and warmth that all the rest of the landscape belies. I have been walking for half an hour. Enough, on this cold day. A short walk is about all I can squeeze out of these woods anyway, so tightly are they pressed between roads and railroad tracks. I can see clear through the leafless mass of trees, picking out hints of yellow siding and red brick on the far side. By stripping away the masking vegetation, winter reminds us what a patchwork the suburbs are, an accumulation of small spaces piled uncertainly together.

As I walk back through the woods toward the house, nose running, teeth chattering, I do not know what I should credit more: the bleakness of the wind and of the lack of birds, or the golden exuberance of the willows; the hard insistence of the pavement all around the woods, or the way my blood seems to warm as the trees scrape the sky, speaking a language we have forgotten.

In June 1862, a month after his untimely death at age forty-four, the *Atlantic Monthly* published Henry David Thoreau's "Walking," a seminal essay in which he issued his famous proclamation "In wildness is the preservation of the world." Writing in Concord, Massachusetts, where he had lived most of his life, Thoreau reported, "I can easily walk ten, fifteen, twenty, any number of miles, commencing at my own door, without going by any house, without crossing a road except where the fox and the mink do: first along by the river, and then the brook, and then the meadow and the wood-side. There are square miles in my vicinity which have no inhabitant. . . . The farmers and their works are scarcely more obvious than woodchucks and their burrows. Man and his affairs, church and state and school, trade and commerce, and manufactures and agriculture, even politics, the most alarming of them all,—I am pleased to see how little space they occupy in the landscape."

This is an experience of wildness that is no longer a possibility in Concord, or in most parts of the country. Most Americans live in cities and suburbs where it is more likely that in a walk of ten or fifteen miles (and who walks that far anymore?) one will cross no extensive tract of wild land. Our towns are parking lots, four-lane highways, strip malls. The countryside is cut into fields and woodlots and fenced-in pastures. Barbed wire slices the Great Plains and the deserts. Clear-cuts shave national forests into blocks. Almost everyone I know of college age or above can relate the same litany of favorite childhood fields and woods and sylvan hideouts converted to buildings or roads. Even where there are parks and preserves they are studded with oft-mowed lawns, cut by roads and trails, littered with discarded bottles and plastic bags.

American suburbs, with their piecemeal grid of grass and asphalt, small remnant woodlots and maintenance-heavy gardens, are becoming an increasingly accurate model of the ecological state of the entire country, and indeed the world. Think of how we've altered the ecological balance of northeastern Illinois in less than two centuries—a blink of an eye in geological time. We have gotten rid of cougars, bears, herds of bison. We have shrunk prairies that once stretched for dozens of miles into small preserves. We have wiped out passenger pigeons and Carolina parakeets for good. We have turned Lake Michigan from a pellucid water teeming with huge sturgeon and lake trout and perch into an enormous uncontrolled experiment in the effects of introduced species: coho salmon, zebra mussels, sea lampreys, alewives. We have muddied rivers and drained marshes. We have built so many houses and roads and malls that anyone who lived in the area a century and a half ago would scarcely recognize it.

Even where large wild places are preserved, elsewhere in North America, the idea that any untouched wilderness remains is a myth. There are places where the human visitor is beyond earshot of cars, trucks, and other machinery; there are some remote and priceless areas in which, from the peak of a mountain, no buildings or roads or jet contrails can be seen. They should remain so. But they are scarcely untouched. Control of predators, the introduction of nonnative plants and animals, air pollution, global warming—these and many other factors have changed, and will continue to change, ecological balances even in places that rarely feel the tread of a Vibram sole. Industrial emissions fall to earth in Arctic snow. Chloroflourocarbons thin the ozone layer, resulting in increased levels of ultraviolet light that kills frogs in remote mountain waters. No place on the surface of the earth can be said to be free of the workings of humanity. If we wish to learn how our lives are mirrored in the natural world—and I would argue that our future well-being, physical and psychological, depends on such learning—we are going to have to do it in landscapes like the suburbs: patches, fragments, a quilt of intensively but inconsistently managed swatches of land.

This is not to say that Thoreau could not find a place to take a good walk in our time. It was not wilderness that he sought, after all, but *wildness,* which can exist comfortably in our cities and suburbs. The weeds pushing open the sidewalk cracks, the coyotes and skunks that roam suburban alleys, the annual winter attack of the flu—these are all signs of a wildness we could not eradicate if we wanted to. Trying to get rid of it is like trying to pop an inflated balloon using only your hands; some of the air escapes your grasp and a pocket seeps out, unpredictably, between two fingers. Wipe out the wolves and the cougars, and the deer will eat the tulips by the front porch. Alter the Great Lakes for the purposes of human commerce, and one morning you find alewives heaped dead on the beach, or zebra mussels clogging the municipal water supply pipe.

And what remains ever and always most fascinating is the wildness within us, which has perhaps not changed all that much since Thoreau's day. This is not a matter of just walking in the woods or of making a hobby out of spotting birds, or wildflowers, or mushrooms; not a matter of a few bird lovers seeing to it that peregrine falcons are nesting on the high cliffs of the Loop and feasting on pigeons fed by retirees in the park. I live in the Southwest now, but a few times a day, every day, I am reminded of my childhood home in northern Illinois by the subtlest of cues: the call of a mourning dove, a certain cast of light, a mild humidity in the air that harks back to long May evenings. The frequency of these memories convinces me that they are not incidental. They are integral elements of my being. These experiences formed the world as it was when and where I first came to know it. They form part of me. They would continue to do so even if I never again visited the place. This is not a question of intellect, but a deep-seated affinity, a matter of spirit, of blood.

When I was eight or nine years old one of my great ambitions was to open a natural history museum. I worked hard at stocking it by collecting natural artifacts of all kinds in the neighboring suburban wilds: feathers, leaves, bones, fragments of birds' eggs—anything I could get my hands on. But the bulk of my collection was made up of what I found on the nearby Lake Michigan beach: fossils, pearly mussel shells, and perfectly smoothed pebbles that came in a million shades of orange and red and gray, some of them almost translucent in the clear water near shore, then drying to a disappointing dullness once indoors.

Storm waves often left shells behind when they washed over the beach. I collected dozens, large and small, pristinely intact or pounded into bits by the waves and rocks. The biggest were four inches long and half as wide, their outsides powdery white or covered with a flaky brown coating. The insides were pearly white and silky smooth. It was hard to resist running my fingers over them again and again.

Infrequently, I found two shell halves still connected by a thin hinge of tough, dark tissue. But the greatest thrill came from finding a still-living mussel, its shapeless copper-gray flesh barely showing between the two almost-closed shell halves. This was a rare event, something that happened only if I was on the beach at just the right moment, before the gulls had had time to scavenge the leavings of the storm waves.

A living mussel was rock-heavy compared to individual shells. I would have loved to keep one in my collection, but it didn't take me long to find out that, kept out of the water, they did not do well at all; they died and dried and decayed and stank up the room. After that I always returned these occasional cast-up mussels to the lake. I have no idea whether they were able to survive, but I liked to think that I was helping them as best I could.

I never did get around to opening that museum. I lost interest; I entered adolescence; I found that each artifact, like those colored pebbles, like the living mussels, could only lose its brightness and potency, its aliveness, after the original moment of gathering it up as a newfound marvel. And so the feathers and bones and rocks and shells gathered dust. Ultimately I threw most of them out. A few I still have: feather of a hawk, tooth of a raccoon, a particularly flawless and glistening shell. Once in a while I take them out and look at them, and sometimes, if I am lucky, a glint of pearl spans the decades and the miles and reminds me of exactly what it was I stooped to pick up.

These essays are the sum of those glints and flashes, fleeting scents on the wind, half-heard rustlings of birds among fallen leaves. They are a record of what remnants of wildness persist in the city and suburbs, in an intensively civilized landscape. They are a reminder of small epiphanies, such as the moment of seeing a wild animal and feeling, in the split second before the intellect knows what is happening, a surge of pure being in the senses, a stirring in the blood. In that moment we are all wild animals, nothing more, nothing less.

It is a stirring I encounter again on this cold March morning, as I walk back through the woods toward my mother's house. Abruptly, over the rasping of the trees, I hear a sound carried on the wind and growing louder—the honking of geese. An uncontrollable, visceral thrill rises in me—surely this is the beginning of spring? My heart pounds a little harder. The sound grows louder, and I spot a ragged V of about twenty geese through the branches. Then another to the north, and a twisted skein of thirty more farther off.

It takes less than a second before I remember that in the suburbs of Chicago flocks of geese are no longer the harbingers of spring they were when I was a boy. It's now a landscape of golf courses and corporate complexes surrounded by lawns and ponds. Hunting, of course, is not allowed. Grass, water, space: it has become a paradise for geese. We couldn't have designed a better one had we tried. And so the geese have learned to stick around all year, in great numbers. Golfers, gardeners, and walkers resent their copious droppings.

I doubt I will ever be able to consider geese pests as so many people do. But with the realization that they are common, and not a sign of spring at all, a little of the pleasure seeps out of hearing them.

The intellectual pleasure, that is. I am sure that all my life I will feel the swift cresting of emotion that runs through the entire body when I hear geese on a raw winter's day. What I am after here, in the essays that follow, is just that: a meeting of head and heart, in the place where joy and sorrow meld into one.

If you stand right fronting and face to face to a fact, you will see the sun glimmer on both its surfaces, as if it were a cimiter, and feel its sweet edge dividing you through the heart and marrow, and so you will happily conclude your mortal career. Be it life or death, we crave only reality.

HENRY DAVID THOREAU
Walden

APRIL: *A Green Heron*

Spring comes grudgingly to the beach, where in April the fog often lies heavy and cold. Lake Michigan is a giant heat sink, absorbing cold all winter long and releasing it slowly through the spring and summer—a quality that is pleasant on hot summer afternoons, but frustrating after a long winter. A half mile west it is often ten or fifteen degrees warmer, and sunnier, on early spring days. Whenever I went to the beach on such days I bundled up in a jacket and tried to find encouragement in the frizzing of green on the myriad shrubs and trees.

One April morning in 1992 the fog had temporarily softened into haze. I sat under the big arborvitae tree that grows where the creek makes its final run over the sand. The sun was a fuzzy, bright disk in the white sky, but I could tell from the way the light was dimming ever so slowly that it was losing its battle with the overcast. Suddenly a crow-sized bird flew in from the north, over the beach, and landed on a dead tree that reached over the creek about twenty yards inland from me.

It was a green heron. Technically it was a "green-backed heron," because the American Ornithologists' Union decreed that to be the bird's official name, changing it from the traditional "green heron," back in 1983. Many beginning birders are somewhat alarmed to find that names and species themselves are not as immutable as field guides seem to imply. New scientific discoveries or theories continually result in the "splitting" of one "species" into two new forms, or the "lumping" of two or more old species into one new one. The result, to those not intimately familiar with the latest scientific discourse, is seemingly arbitrary name changes that often fly in the face of long-cherished tradition.

In 1993, because of new discoveries, or at least new opinions, in genetics and taxonomy, the ornithologists returned to the original name of "green heron," which was fine with me since I'd never left off the habit of calling the bird that anyway. And there on the creek it didn't seem to make much difference. True, the heron's back and upper wing feathers are colored deep jade, at least part of the time. In full sun I'd seen a green heron's back glow tropical emerald, like a parrot. But when the bird turned slightly toward me it could have been called a slate-gray heron. And that was only the beginning. The heron's legs were pale chartreuse, its beak brilliant cadmium yellow. Its breast appeared rich rufous at first, but as a particularly thick patch of haze passed under the sun it turned into a pinkish purple, a color so dark and rich that it seemed lit from within, as if the heron were made of some rare marble, half crystal, half opaque.

The heron posed stiff as a stick, unmoving. It was perfect, discrete.

It was, I thought, full of itself. Its body was chunky, its neck thick where it arose from the chest, but the beak was honed to such a perfect point, sharp and deadly, that it was as if the heron encompassed all the paradoxes and ambiguities of the world—rounded and straight; an individual animal yet fully part of its ecosystem; a predator, as much fish, really, as bird. The heron was magnificent in its stillness, its waiting. It conceded no superiority. By its very presence it proved that there is no higher calling than to be a heron.

I opened my journal and began writing this down. Rufous, pinkish purple—what color was the breast? None of the words I found conveyed the richness of what I saw. Nothing I wrote could convey the essence of that bird, that living creature perched on dead branches. Writing about it was like trying to stuff a live animal into a paper bag. Green heron, green-backed heron—it made no difference. Neither phrase was right. Neither could capture the glint in the bird's eye, which I saw as an awareness, as another consciousness, looking at the world, looking at me, aware that it was unlike me. What could do justice to that look?

My efforts seemed even more inadequate when I looked at the bird's surroundings. When I looked closely, the fuzz of emerging green resolved itself into an infinitude of new leaves, each perfectly self-contained, each reflecting the sky's light in endlessly varied hues that ruffled and rustled with the wind's breath. Every twig branched in a new direction; every trunk revealed the scarring and individual nature of each tree's story. There was no way to do justice to the scene in what I wrote.

Through my journal-writing I wanted not only to be able to remember the scene later; I wanted to be forced to look more closely. And I suppose I was, description being a test of what one has seen. "We think we have looked at a thing sharply until we are asked for its specific features," wrote the naturalist John Burroughs. I needed to look closely at the heron's breast to see whether it was rufous or purple, but even after I had decided on the best possible word, I knew that its specific meaning failed to pin down the visual impression.

Each of those words—each of these words—was a translation that only imperfectly conveyed the original meaning of what was said out there, on the creek, between the heron and my retina and brain, in this little snippet of the endless conversation of the world.

The word *world* comes from an ancient Germanic root, *wer*, that refers, according to the Oxford English Dictionary, to the "age or life of man." Thus when we speak of the "world," we are not speaking of the totality of the planet we live upon, but rather of the human perception of the place. "World" is the planet as it relates to us; it does not necessarily describe whatever it is the heron sees with its sharp eyes. When we speak of "seeing the world," the implication is that the traveler has come into contact with a good deal of what makes up our common home. We tend to overlook the limited nature of that sight, assuming that things are as we see them.

As I sat by the creek, stymied in my writing, I wondered what it is we really see. The colors of the heron were memorable, but experienced birders know that color is among a bird's most deceptive identifying characteristics, because it is so variable. On a more heavily shaded bank the green heron's back could have been blue-gray. A bluebird is gray or brown whenever the sky is heavily overcast, as the brilliant gorget of the male ruby-throated hummingbird is a dull black until sunlight hits it just right. Color is not an absolute but rather an endlessly complicated interaction between matter, light, and the nerve endings in our eyes.

This is not just a matter of appearances but a substantial fact about the way we perceive the world—namely, incompletely. The human eye has only a limited (albeit large) number of rods and cones that transfer information from light waves toward the brain. There is a virtually infinite amount of visual information in a scene like that along the creek. There is no way we can take it all in. And so seeing is a matter of simplifying multiplicity by fudging the details. Seeing is the practice of learning to focus on particular elements of a scene. Seeing is honest deceit. Seeing is itself a language, a shorthand that allows us to navigate. We never really see what *is*; we see our own version of reality. We see the world.

To understand how limited our own vision is, consider bald eagles, which are believed to be able to detect the movement of potential prey up to three miles away. Or owls, some of which are able to spot mice six feet away at a light level equivalent to that obtained by standing 1,170 feet from a single candle. Try that sometime, if you can find a place that's dark enough. We humans have some seven million cones—which are associated with seeing daylight and color—in each retina; some eagles and hawks pack that many into each square millimeter of retina. It's a matter of hardware, of being able to process more information.

Not only higher animals see what we do not. Bees use ultraviolet light to find flowers. Many insects orient themselves by detecting the polarization of light, which tells them where the sun is by looking at even a small patch of blue sky on an overcast day. Dragonflies, whose eyes have thousands of individual facets, can take in movement more than ten times as fast as that which we can perceive. To a dragonfly, a Hollywood movie, whose multiple frames per second mimic the speed of life as we perceive it, would seem absurdly sluggish, more so than the slow-motion replay of a football highlight is to us.

The incompleteness that imbues the way we see our surroundings has been underlined by the startling discoveries of physicists exploring quantum mechanics—if it makes sense to speak of "discoveries" when the realm of subatomic particles the scientists are exploring is not visible and cannot possibly be made visible to us. You might say they have not been discovering anything, but simply coming up with new metaphors that seek to explain what reality is. They have "discovered," for example, that the light bouncing back at me from the heron's back consists of particles. They have also discovered that it consists of waves. The rules of physics state that it is not possible for light to be both wave and particle. Yet it can be either, depending on which way we measure it. In other words, our sight is not just incomplete; it also structures what we are looking at in a particular way. What is observed is not safely separable from the observer. As Werner

Heisenberg, the German physicist who was one of the architects of the deconstruction of classical physics, wrote, "What we observe is not nature itself, but nature exposed to our method of questioning."

In any case, it does us no good to dwell on abilities we lack. Consider, as did the writer R. H. Smythe, that "eyes which become too efficient might cause problems and raise their owner a deal of embarrassment." Or think of what we can do that other animals cannot. Many of the most sharp-eyed hunters, including members of the dog family and many birds, are curiously unable to see prey animals in plain sight if they are not moving. "Frogs and toads," one authority has written about a particularly cold-blooded experiment, "can starve to death while surrounded by dead flies which are, of course, motionless."

According to evolutionary principles, we are suited to see that which helps us to survive. In the case of humans, that includes such items as bright-colored and nutritious fruits; animals of a size worth hunting; dangerous predators; landscapes with water and trees. One of the happiest results of our lengthy evolution, to my mind, is that we are well suited to see birds.

That spring, each week brought new arrivals from the south. One week there were song sparrows poking in the duff of driftwood logs; later, northern waterthrushes skulked on the creek mud. Shorebirds scuttled swiftly on the sand, their tracks wiped out by every next wave. As the foliage expanded, olive-green Tennessee warblers and brilliant scarlet tanagers showed up high in the treetops, hopping from branch to branch like wind-tossed leaves. With every new week, with each rise in the length of the day or in temperature, I saw more species.

I noticed myself becoming better at it—not necessarily at identifying the birds I saw but rather at spotting them, period. I was becoming more aware of small movements, distant dots in the sky, small incongruities against a backdrop of sand or fallen leaves. That's the best thing about bird-watching: paying attention to birds forces an observer to constantly push the sensory envelope. There is always a bird flying by so high or so far off that you can, with practice, just guess what it might be; and beyond that another so distant that it is impossible to say for certain that it is a bird and not a leaf whirling high in the wind, or a balloon strayed from someone's birthday party or used-car sale. There is always some commotion going on in the downed leaves. There is always movement half-glimpsed out of the corner of your eye in the shrubs, a faint impression that vanishes when you look directly—just as the Pleiades can best be seen with a glance slightly off-center.

This is what I am always looking for, the edges of perception. An unknown bird dips behind the trees on the ridge. In the leaves somewhere is a rustling so faint it is drowned by the pounding of blood in my ears. I hold my breath. I strain. The rustling is gone, a shadow of desire. Migration is a great wave that passes by twice a year, but it is made up of so many individual frailties that it is easy to miss. When you stop to really watch and listen for the endless tiny movements that constitute the migration of birds, it is like waking in the dark silence of midnight and hearing no other sound but that of a lover's breath, absolutely regular and absolutely vulnerable.

What is it we are looking for when we look at birds? I can't help but think this: it is a matter of hanging on. Each spring, the migration goes by so quickly; the seasons pass, the years fade, children grow up, subdivisions mushroom from fields, and in this whirlwind of change the presence of a single green heron is a rock-solid fact. However imperfect the words I have to describe it, however partial my view of it, that bird is right there in front of me now, filling my thoughts. It is something whole, complete. It is enough.

What we choose to hang on to doesn't have to be a bird. I met a biologist once who had studied horned lizards in the Arizona desert. The best way to find horned lizards, he told me, is to walk the silty creosote flats, head down, looking for their scat: quarter-inch-thick cylinders that glitter with the hard exoskeletons of ants. As we talked his eyes scanned the ground, restless. After years of looking for lizard droppings, could he focus on anything else? Every time he'd found a pellet it was a victory, a concrete goal attained in the midst of endless multiplicity. Lizard droppings became one of his world's organizing principles.

One could decry this as artificiality: because most of us now live at a considerable remove from immediate reliance on nature, because we no longer need to be able to read the weather or game trails, we make up tasks for ourselves in the outdoors. We catalog, we make lists, we tally what we have found. We categorize. We monitor and measure and map. We ignore much of the complexity around us and focus on particular objects of desire: lizard scat, songbirds, native wildflowers. We want a handle on our surroundings. We want desperately to feel at home. For whatever reasons, more and more of us are looking at birds on the beach or at the feeder, restoring prairies, spending our vacation time watching bears in Alaska or whales in Hawaii. These activities are laudable, but I cannot help but think that they are in part a distorted reflection of something we lost along the way. At some point, in generations past, we lost the heron's easy familiarity with its surroundings, its absolute acceptance, and now we are expending a great deal of energy on the inchoate desire to have it back.

What we are acting out is the shape and the feel of absence—and not just the absence of intimacy, but also the absence of specific creatures. Wander and watch the woods of the Midwest long enough, and the ever-lonesome calls of mourning doves seem to become faint echoes of the passenger pigeons that are now irrevocably gone. Don't the ripe acorns dropping from the white oaks conjure up thoughts of the bears that once fattened for hibernation on this rich food? Can you look at skeins of waterfowl heading north in early spring without realizing that they reflect the passage of now-rare whooping cranes or Eskimo curlews? There is much we have lost in the suburbs, in the Midwest, in all our land.

Here are just a few of the animals lost from Illinois; residents of any other state could write a similar list. The Carolina parakeet. The ivory-billed woodpecker. Free-roaming buffalo, *Bison bison*. Cougar, black bear, and elk. The passenger pigeon and its endemic chewing louse, *Columbicola extinctus*. The Dakota skipper, mustard white, Diana fritillary, and brown lacewing, among many other insects. The lusty crayfish. The catspaw, leafshell, round combshell, long-solid, and other freshwater mussels. The alligator gar. The hellbender. The broad-banded watersnake. The gray wolf and porcupine. Crystal, harlequin, gilt, and stargazing darters. There are more. There are getting to be more every year.

And there is a place, or a frame of mind, in which we can experience our perception of their absence anew, each time we go outdoors. It is a place at the edge of sight or hearing, where the fine line between presence and absence seems to swell into a gray area and a tantalizing uncertainty rules the senses. We encounter a finely drawn mixture of hope and doubt here, as the familiarity of the quotidian mingles with the longing for the absolutely unpredictable. A rare bird can fly into your backyard on the most ordinary of days. This is in large measure the pleasure and challenge of watching for birds: they, more than other animals, tend to show up in unexpected places—a snowy owl at the airport, a goshawk in the woodlot by the school. Birding centers on the surprise, the unknown. Each new bird that I half-sensed in the bushes or in the far distance, as I sat by the arborvitae tree, was an invocation of possibility that, at least for a moment, seemed absolute and unlimited. If an oddly colorful heron could show up here, why not an Eskimo curlew? And so I did not mind that some birds disappeared without my discovering what they were; in my ignorance they could have been anything, anything at all.

One spring day I noticed this: when you hear them far off, when they are so distant that you have to question whether you are hearing birds or your imagination, the raucous cries of crows sound sweet.

Whether my glass is half empty or half full depends on the day, on my mood. Any number of circumstances have the power to remind me that there remains much to celebrate, including the gaudy certitude of a certain green heron. If such a sight is a reminder of what we are missing, it is also incontrovertible evidence that even the incomplete riches we perceive all around us, every day, are immeasurable.

Which is why, when the heron flapped off its branch and flew off the same way it had come, I felt a fine sense of contentment. It was beautiful. What else can I tell you?

. . . The way I feel about the Midwest is the way my skin feels and the way I feel my own skin—in layers and broad stripes and shades, in planes and in the periphery. The Midwest as hide, an organ of sense and not power, delicate and coarse at the same time. The Midwest transmits in fields and waves. It is the place of sense. It sometimes differentiates heat and cold, pain and pleasure, but most often registers the constant bombardment, the monotonous feel of feeling. Living here on the great flat plain teaches you a soft touch, since sensation arrives in huge sheets, stretched tight, layer upon layer, another kind of flood.

MICHAEL MARTONE
"The Flatness"

MAY: *Clay*

We called the place "the clay hills." I was a kid at the time, eight and nine and ten years old. The clay hills were the lakeside face of a steep bluff, a sharp sliver of clay that rose up over the beach like a breaking wave. They were our play-ground, the steepest and roughest and most uncared-for place around, a far cry from the manicured lawns of the neighboring North Shore suburbs. This was where we could let loose. We'd climb recklessly to the top, grabbing on to the roots that stuck out of the clay like dead hands, bruising shins as a knob of clay gave way. We'd light fires just to see what would happen. We engaged in skirmishes and battles fueled by dirt clods, without fear of having our parents stalk out of the house and demand that we clean up after ourselves, as happened each time we did the same in the driveway or street. At least once, I remember, we were inspired to fill a half-dozen garbage bags with the empty beer cans left after teenage parties. When it was wet we tracked the bluff's sticky mud indoors, grit lodged under our fingernails and on our kneecaps.

At first glance the bluff looked drab, uniform, a steep-canted slope of dull earth. Its crest was an undulating lip of living forest soil, knit together with roots, that overswept the edge like a wave's foam. Below was the surging face, bulging under its own weight, pitched at forty-five to sixty degrees and largely bare of vegetation.

From a boat it was a long, ugly gash amid the verdant green of the lakefront. But a closer look revealed subtle gradations. It was colored every tone from a steely battleship gray to a blond tan that deepened to rich chocolate brown when wet. In broad sunlight it became a desert dun too bright to look at without squinting. The most barren stretches were punctuated only by lone spikes of goldenrod, clover, thistle. Here and there large patches of topsoil would fall in slow motion from the top of the bluff, miniature continental plates, colliding and splitting, sliding at a pace measured in months or years, bearing their living cargoes down to the next winter's surf. Some carried, upright, red oaks and hornbeams up to twenty feet tall. The wreckage of other trees that had already fallen littered the beach until it was carried off by high waves.

The clay came in a number of grades. There must be sound geological descriptions suited to its gradations in color and texture, but I am not versed in them. As a boy I made my own classifications, drawn by the intimacy of touch. There was clay that lay fallen in sharp, hard-edged chunks on the beach during dry spells, masquerading as rock but quick to grow smooth and rounded once pounded by swells. When the waves washed it into the lake it formed small globules just offshore, squishing between our toes when we waded barefoot, liable to be embedded with mussel shells, colorful pebbles, smoothed bits of opaque glass, beetle carapaces, fish scales, old coins, bottle caps, and all the other detritus that washed up on the beach. There was clay that dangled in vase-shaped clods from exposed tree roots on the ridge, sheltered from rain by the mat of topsoil, luring crows and blue jays that would land on the roots, sway pendulously to a stop, gaze about, then fly off again. There was clay that ran a viscous gray liquid in March, turned to slurry by the seeps that arose at the end of winter and marked unseen stratifications inside the bluff. It ran down the slope like wet cement, piling up in lovely, cone-shaped alluvial fans that glistened like ectoplasm and moved more slowly than a winter-muddled turtle. When I was a boy I could never resist poking holes in it with a stick and watching them fill again so slowly, so deliberately; or chucking rocks in for the sake of the succulent *splat!* and the spatter of gray droplets showering the sand; or, once, upon finding a plastic toy tugboat washed ashore, positioning it bow-down in the soft mud, riding the swell, surfing on a gray wave powered by all the weight of a mountain.

That's how I remember the bluff, as a place that fell outside the precise categories of the street above—pavement, lawn, shrubbery, garden, house. The bluff was different, rough, disordered, beyond the boundaries. It didn't belong to anyone in particular. Each winter chunks of it crashed or melted down into the surf. It changed shape, presenting a new landscape each spring. It was its own place, unlike any other.

The adults on the block were the ones who had to worry about the clay hills. They had to pony up so that the neighborhood association could afford liability insurance in case one of us reckless children broke a leg, or a neck. The bluff was anarchy in action, the geographic version of an eight-year-old high on sugar. Best to stay away from it. Which to us was all the more reason to go.

It wasn't until some years later that I understood that the bluff was not anarchic at all. It may not have obeyed the Western laws which hold that property is fixed and immutable, but it did obey laws of its own, namely the strictures of geology and erosion that were responsible for the creation of the environment I knew as a child. Like much of the upper Midwest, it was a relic of the Ice Age. Twenty-five thousand years ago, as the great Wisconsinian glacier ground its slow course through what is now Michigan, Wisconsin, Illinois, it picked up the topmost layer of the terrain it crossed: rocks, soil, sand, tree trunks, bones. When it finally melted, ten thousand years later, it left all that duff behind, crumbled and ground to varied consistencies. Much of the sand and silt and clay and gravel wound up in moraines, which marked the boundaries where lobes of the glacier melted. Up to a hundred feet high, they still crinkle the flat land with their sinuous ridges. What we called the clay hills was only a small part of the long face of a moraine exposed to the lake.

By the time American settlers got there early in the nineteenth century, the miles-long moraine along the lakefront sported an open forest of stately oaks and hickories, with maples in the ravines, that must have looked as if it had stood there forever. "The rugged bluff, one hundred feet high, the deep ravines, and charming groves, make it one of the most picturesque spots in the west," effused the *Chicago Times*. The area began sprouting farms and villages as the future city of Chicago began pulling itself out of the muck to the south, in the 1830s and 1840s.

The forests, with their big trees, must have given the settlers a false sense of permanence. In fact, the bluffs and beaches were part of a finely tuned and ever-changing natural system fueled by perennial destruction and change. This is how it worked: Much of the sand and gravel pulled from bluffs during storms did not vanish for good into the lake's depths but was washed up on shore, forming wide beaches. Along the lake's western edge the waves most often blow in from the north or northeast; they bounce off the shore in a southeasterly direction. The waves and their reflections combine to form a current that moves south just offshore, known as the longshore current. Since the glacier melted, sand grains first deposited in the bluffs had slowly moved south on the longshore current, stopping on one beach for a couple of years, on a sandbar for a season, on another beach for a human lifespan, before finally reaching the extensive dunes at the lake's south end. The aggregate effect was that of a great river of sand moving south in fits and starts, all fed by the bluffs that gave way, slumped, and washed into the lake during storms. From the time the glacier melted to the time white settlement began, the shoreline probably receded inland at least a mile. The dunes down south grew enormous.

That's how the system worked, but like many natural cycles it became unacceptable once the land was parceled out into lots, particularly once wealthy Chicagoans decided that the lakefront bluffs made fine sites for summer homes and, later, year-round residences. The land became too valuable to be eroded away. Owners began fortifying their holdings by building seawalls of rock, steel, or concrete to protect fragile bluffs and beaches from battering waves. They built steel seawalls known as groins out into the lake to trap a bit of the sand carried south on the great longshore river.

The effect was to begin a sort of arms race, for every one of these projections into the lake trapped sand on its north side and interrupted the flow of the river. A landowner whose neighbor to the north built a groin had little choice but to build one of his own to trap the little sand that moved around the first; otherwise waves would scour out his beach, and the current was not carrying enough material anymore to rebuild it. Beaches that had once stretched for miles, split only by occasional bluff blowouts, were transformed into endless pocket-sized scallops of sand, each one nestled on the north side of a wall of rock or steel. The situation was exacerbated by the federal government, which in the 1880s built a harbor at Waukegan, some fifteen miles to the north, and found that it had to build enormously long groins to keep the harbor mouth from filling in. The groin on the north side of its entrance channel trapped so much sand that within the next hundred years some bluffs to the south receded up to four hundred feet.

The history of Great Lakes beaches is further complicated by climate cycles that govern water levels. In the 1960s, when my beachgoing began, Lake Michigan was at its lowest level in over a century. Beaches were wide. By the time my family moved into a house near the clay hills, in 1971, the delicate balance between precipitation and evaporation had shifted. The lakes began to rise, and remained high through the 1970s. Beaches shrank, bluffs were gnawed away. Across the lake, where dunes fronted the shore, houses slipped down loose slopes and into the water. These were good years for the companies that built seawalls and groins. More shoreline owners invested in armor. Everywhere the lakefront was defended with steel and rock. The flow of sediment must have been at an all-time low; Chicago and other municipalities maintained their beaches only by trucking in vast amounts of sand every spring. Many beaches were scarcely large enough for a towel and picnic basket. Often it was virtually impossible to walk any distance along the beach; the way was blocked by high steel groins and by reaches where deep water stood at the foot of seawalls.

The beach below the clay hills was in particularly bad shape: it was always narrow and sometimes vanished entirely during storms. Waves battered the clay and the water turned concrete gray. The bluff was unusual because it was the only one for miles not protected by a seawall or groin. No house was at risk, so no one bothered armoring it; it would have been too expensive. And so the bluff kept eroding, an eternal sore that never had the chance to scab over with new grass and wildflowers and red cedars before the next series of storms came.

The swallows arrived while I was in high school, and after that they showed up around the first of May every year. They excavated a large colony in the barren clay. It was near the ravine, at the bluff's southern tip, where a patch of the eroded face showed yellow and sandy. The clay here was coarse and friable, yet it was able to hold a steeper angle of repose than the surrounding iron-gray sediment, so that its face was almost vertical. In morning sunlight it glowed gold. In this place the swallows dug their burrows, pocking about a hundred silver-dollar-sized holes, just wider than they were high, into a space perhaps twenty-five feet long and eight or ten high. Immediately above the colony several red oaks stood on the brink. The topsoil held together by their roots shielded the burrows from rain, while the dangling roots themselves served as perches.

The bank swallows' swift and darting flight signaled the beginning of warm weather—insect season. With quick strokes of their scimitar wings they cut the air over the lake, always flocking together in gangs and skeins, catching flying insects or dipping low to drink on the wing.

They were a perfect match to the color of the bluff's clay. A thin, dark chest band of the same brown-gray as their backs and wings slashed their white underparts. In early May I watched them beginning to excavate burrows. They reused old ones, too, but slabs of the sandy clay tended to fall each winter, necessitating new construction. They fluttered to a landing, clung to minute clay perches with their tiny, weak feet, scratched at the clay with their short bills. It was difficult to imagine how they dug out entire burrows, which grew deep, their ends hidden in shadow.

Later in May I watched the swallows alighting on the beach, where they picked up matchstick-sized pieces of driftwood with their beaks and flew off toward the burrows. They were irascible. Often one swallow flew directly at another perching on the bluff. Upon impact, the two tumbled together down the slope for as much as several yards, each flying off as it regained equilibrium. They tussled in the air, too, by twos and threes, in a whirling, chirping confusion of wings that often as not landed on the beach, from which the combatants flew off again and resumed chasing one another. I don't know whether these encounters were manifestations of fighting, or courtship, or just the raw exuberance of spring given flight; the latter is what it looked like when they occasionally swarmed over the beach all together, eighty or a hundred of them. They retreated toward their burrows, then gusted down the slope and over the water like a great blast of dry leaves on a windy autumnal street.

By June the birds had settled into parental duties. They foraged singly, in pairs, or in small groups, flying either over the trees, trailing long strings of twitterings, or just over the water or beach. They flew near me, swerving over the creek mouth, and always I was impressed at how muscular they appeared at close range. They worked their wings hard. Swallows had always seemed effortless flyers to me, but here they were pumping and hustling like athletes. They caught beakfuls of insects and returned to the bluff to feed their nestlings. They pulled up, slowed at the last instant, and disappeared into a burrow, then reappeared a few moments later, diving out, falling in a curving trajectory for a few feet, then catching themselves and flying off to hunt more.

There was no way to watch the swallows without feeling cheered by this energetic life forming itself out of gnats and mosquitoes. I was glad of their twittering and of their close-serried burrows. I thought of the glaciers laying down their burden of naked clay and sand, of the slow march of vegetation that covered it—first the tiny, tough, tundra flowers, the scrub willows, the spruces, the birches, then the pines and maples and oaks and hornbeams, the creeping honeysuckles, blue asters, woodland sunflowers—and for a moment I was of the Ice Age too. Here came the first bands of hunters wandering north after mammoths or long-horned bison; they paused to look at the tribe of newly arrived swallows that dug their burrows in raw banks of clay, having migrated farther north than ever before to feast on the fresh-hatched insects of meltwater lakes. I walked, humbled, across a landscape on which the marks of humanity had fallen as comfortably as those burrows folded into the clay, as appropriate, as temporary, in surroundings wrought by masses of ice so big and so deep they must have defied imagination and become myth as soon as human eyes fell upon them. Whenever the swallows dug out a new burrow, flipping the ancient grains out with quick pecks of the bill, the Ice Age was still a living memory. Its remnants crumbled away daily, distilling new life each year out of climate and geography and the swift rush of wings.

My parents sold the place after my sisters and I moved out; they bought a smaller house nearby. But I still go back to look at the bluff about twice a year. I'm happy to report that the swallows are still there; when they arrive in spring to find their old burrows eroded away they simply excavate new ones. They're easy, adaptable, bound to the bluff itself but not to any individual nest.

I like to go back. I like to watch the swallows swarm and to remember how generations of the birds have been doing the same thing in the same place. I like to see the yellow-orange goldenrods and the sapphire asters dotting the sloping face of the bluff, spots of brilliant color in a field of gray and tan. I like to see the oak roots dangling above, knowing that they belong to trees that were well inside the woods years ago. I like to imagine how much the bluff has given way to the water, which is the one thing I can look at that seems truly not to have changed.

In twenty-five years the bluff has receded thirty, forty, fifty feet, perhaps more. I really don't know how far it has traveled. My legs and the gaps under my fingernails remember the gritty feel of clay, my nose is reminded on each visit of the bright, startling smell that comes when a piece of clay is shattered into dust, but my eyes cannot stamp the contours of land on what is now water. The bluff is a visible testimony to change, but my memory cannot retain that vanished turf. Time erodes the landscape of memory, leaving murkiness, haze, a past half-imagined. And so every time I visit I look at the water and at the diminished bluff, and always I find myself wondering what other landscapes lie out there on the glittering water, rising to wind and sunshine only in the memory of the dead.

When I return I seek out things I can hang on to. Once, just before I moved away, on a raw winter day, I saw a coyote loping along the lip of the bluff and then down onto the sand. It was the first one I'd ever seen in the suburbs. They were coming back. I followed the tracks all along the beach below the clay hills and found two that were crisply outlined in half-liquid mud.

I hurried back to the house. Naturalists suggest plaster of paris for casting track impressions, but I couldn't find any. Instead I found a box of hydraulic cement from one of my father's long-ago repair projects. I hustled back down to the beach, mixed the powder up with lake water in an old jam jar, and poured it gently onto the mud. Late that afternoon I came back. One of the soft cement chunks broke when I tried to pry it out of the track, but the other one held. I carried it inside and let it dry by the heat of a lightbulb. I still have it.

Now I turn the impression over in my hands, feeling its contours. The pads are gritty, rough, like sand. I compare them to a coyote pelt my mother gave me. Her father brought it back from a trip out west during the Great Depression, before coyotes had become suburban animals in the Midwest. I hold the cement track impression next to the front paw of that long-dead coyote, whose pelt is still extraordinarily soft and silky. I compare the two, back and forth, the two like animals frozen into stunted versions of immortality, and I reflect on how I never knew my grandfather and so I have no idea, no idea at all really, why he chose to bring this particular relic back from the West.

But I think I can guess.

Cicada—did it
chirp till it
knew nothing else?
BASHŌ

JUNE: *Cicadas*

By the middle of June the sound of cicadas singing was a solid wall. You could open the door and walk right into it. It could stun you awake.

It had grown only gradually. At first it was a background buzz difficult to distinguish from the ordinary humming of crickets, bees, and flies. On overcast days you could barely hear it; a cool breeze wiped it out. As the days wound into June the sun nourished the sound, unfolding it like a leaf, until on hot days it seemed less a noise than a deep vibration, rising and falling like a wave. It grew and faded with the temperature, wind, sunshine, and your own distance from the big trees. On the hottest afternoons it was a caterwauling, a crescendo in the deep woods. It was a roaring as loud as a train. Cicadas were singing on every leaf and bough, twig and branch. An entomologist once went to study cicadas in a floodplain forest near Chicago. "The sound was so intense," he wrote, "that two persons face to face in this woods could not hear each other talk."

And sometimes the insects surprised us and kept up their wailing all night. Weaned of the sun, the buzzing continued, independent at last of the darkened ground.

⌒

Cicadas are more patient than we; they lie still so long, and then who could begrudge them their one noisy chance at living? Several vivid images of their last emergence crowd my memory. One night I drove home late and found cicadas covering the ravine bridge near the driveway. They swarmed in the big pools of light cast by the streetlights. They danced round one another in an intricate way, reminding me of the tiny windup toys in a battery commercial. I regretted having to drive home because it meant crushing so many of them. But it seemed there would be endless numbers more to take their place.

When I rode on the bike trail through the forest preserve cicadas fell from overhanging branches and littered the ground. It was all I could do, if I was to make any speed at all, just to avoid the pairs copulating. I figured if they'd waited so long they deserved that privilege, at least.

In town that spring much of the talk was of cicadas. They are coming, reported the newspapers. Scientists echoed resonant names— *Magicicada cassini*, *Magicicada septendecim*—and claimed that an acre of rich bottomland forest could produce a ton of cicada flesh, a better yield than a cattle pasture. In the hardware store people traded tips on how to keep them out of the landscaping. There was a certain uneasiness to this talk. Cicadas didn't fit into summer vacation plans. "Seventeen-year locusts," they are commonly called—an unfortunate label, for who can think of locusts without the swarms of the Bible coming to mind? "For they covered the face of the whole earth, so that the land was darkened; and they did eat every herb of the land, and all the fruit of the trees which the hail had left: and there remained not any green thing in all the trees, nor in the herbs of the field."

It was not like that at all. If locusts—which are grasshoppers—are the scourge of God, cicadas are the dolls: brightly colored, harmless, precious. They can be comically clumsy. They are not afraid of us. In their abundance they can seem absolutely absurd. They were a thrill for me at age ten; now, at twenty-seven, I was enthralled. I waited for their emergence like a kid anticipating Christmas.

Before most of us ever see them, they have been living underground for seventeen years. They grow with almost geological slowness. Like other insects of the order Homoptera, they are vegetarians, and their diet is liquid. Homopterans—the order includes treehoppers, planthoppers, leafhoppers, froghoppers, whiteflies, aphids, and scale insects, as well as cicadas—attach their sharp mouthparts to root or branch and become, in effect, a backwater in the flow of sap from roots to foliage. The pressure that draws water and nutrients up toward the green leaves is great enough that the insects need hardly exert themselves. They just hang on while the nutrients flow through. Sometimes their main exertion is to limit the flow of sap so their bodies do not burst.

The sap is rich in carbohydrates, which furnish quick energy that cicadas and other homopterans do not need. And so they excrete the excess—a sweet waste material called honeydew. At times it builds up in thick layers, most notably where scale insects have attached themselves to exposed leaves and branches. The honeydew of the tamarisk manna scale is particularly sweet, and is deposited in particularly large quantities. Today, as in biblical times, residents of Arabia and Iraq collect it as a delicacy: manna not from heaven, but from the earth. "And when the dew that lay was gone up, behold, upon the face of the wilderness there lay a small, round thing, as small as the hoar frost on the ground. . . . It was like coriander seed, white; and the taste of it was like wafers made with honey."

Cicadas leave no such easy treasure. They attach themselves to roots a foot or two underground and pass their honeydew directly into the soil. They are a conduit from root to soil, a part of the tree, moving no faster than the roots themselves. In a healthy, moist woodland the roots of a single large oak or maple might feed up to forty thousand cicada nymphs. That's up to one and a half million cicadas per acre: think of how sweet the soil must become.

They grow slowly and so harm their host tree little, if at all, instead swelling on the tree's accumulated surplus of soil and sun and rain. By their twelfth year they are almost full-grown, about the size of a cashew. But they stay buried another five years, perhaps allowing any laggards among them to catch up. Even growth this slow can't be accomplished through sap alone, because it lacks proteins. Cicadas have large bodies to build, and so, like peas and clovers, they harbor in their bodies colonies of bacteria that are able to fix soil-borne nitrogen, which in turn helps synthesize proteins. One day we will probably learn that the tree can't live without the cicadas umbilically tied into its roots, growing like wood all summer and hibernating in the winter. The bacteria are to the cicada as the cicadas are to the tree—how can we say where one living body ends and another begins?

So all the Insect People began to fly around in great circles and swarms, and then they spiraled upward to the sky of the first world, looking for a place to fly through it to the upper land. They flew around it for a long time before they found a small opening to the east. It was as narrow and crooked as the tendril of a vine, but they managed to crawl through this opening and found themselves on the muddy surface of the second world.

MARGARET SCHEVILL LINK
*The Pollen Path: A Collection of Navajo Myth*s

How do we know when to be born? Who will tell us what imponderable message causes the cicadas to climb out of their burrows (how well must they know them!) to seek the open air? Think about this: They have been down there for over eight hundred and seventy-five weeks. Their lives are almost done. It is now time for a change.

In the northern Midwest it is typically late May before the rains are warm enough to cajole the cicadas upward. Then the showers pull the nymphs to the surface as surely as the emergent sun, poking through a wrack of clouds, pulls mist from the steaming soil. Often all the cicadas in an area emerge almost synchronously in the course of a single evening. They crawl slowly out of the little holes they have dug up from their burrows. In parts of the vegetable garden, that year, there were easily a hundred holes for every square foot. The nymphs are an inch long and sheathed in a glossy brown armor. They crawl about as cumbersomely as tiny tanks. Each crawls until it finds a shrub, or a tree trunk, or a brick wall on which it can plant a firm grip. The skin splits right down the middle, and each cicada laboriously walks out of its skin, head first, long abdomen last.

The adult that emerges from this metamorphosis is called by entomologists an imago, after the Latin for "image," and indeed they are beautiful enough to seem at first—in their newly minted perfection—more image than reality. On warm days in late May and early June I could see, no matter where I walked, the new imagos, still glistening, waiting to take off. I thought I had never seen such elegant insects. Their long and gently rounded wings were crisp, straight, translucent, sharply veined in orange shading to black toward the tips; their bodies shiny, hard, and black; their legs orange-brown. Their eyes were like brilliant-red trade beads. They measured about an inch and a half from eyes to the tips of their folded wings.

The brief period of transformation from nymph to imago is fraught with dangers, not the least of which is the threat of being eaten while the insect is not yet very mobile. Like a new butterfly's, their wings are wet when they emerge from the nymphal skin. It takes an hour or two for the adult's blood pressure to inflate the wings to full size; then they dry and harden. At times something goes wrong. I saw many whose wings had not set properly. On some both wings looked like shriveled leaves. Or the left might be fully extended, but the right crumpled into a ball. There were infinite variations, but in the end it meant only that these insects would never get off the ground. They would have to walk, seeking a mate on foot until their inevitable end in bird's beak or chipmunk's teeth.

Cicadas mate high in the trees. Whether an individual reproduces successfully depends on a successful metamorphosis and a solid pair of wings. Those that are crippled are, in this Darwinian world, almost certainly washed up, superfluous. They can do everything but fly, but it's unlikely they will ever reproduce. Do they lose hope, give themselves willingly up to beak or claw? Or do they become laughing and crazy Zen monks of the insect world, sharing a secret joke too obtuse for the rest of us? Do they care? They seem to just keep on doing what they have been getting ready all their lives to do. There is a blind resilience to the insect world that horrifies more easily than it inspires. Should we take comfort in thinking that it is only we humans who perceive an injustice in a world that so blithely dashes seventeen years of waiting in an hour? When do our own wings harden? For what moment in the sun do we live?

At rest, a cicada's long wings extend beyond the pointed tip of the abdomen. The petal-shaped wings we see cover the smaller, rear pair of wings until the insect takes flight. These rear wings are as wide as the forewings—hence their name homopteran, meaning "like-winged"—and as translucent and boldly veined. When cicadas take flight they are heavy-bodied, cumbersome, able to cover only short distances. They'll launch themselves into space with what looks to a human eye like faith, for how can wings so transparent support a body so massive? But they manage; on calm days I could see them rising throughout the woods in long curving arcs, sunlight glinting on their wings. Sometimes the heaviness of their bodies seemed to overcome their best efforts, and they spiraled down and down until they hit something, smacking into tree trunks with a hearty *click*.

When I was a boy I learned how to climb trees on the big arborvitae near the beach. Its branches stepped upward just like a ladder and took my best friend and me high enough to get a good view of the beach and the tree-lined ravine—high enough that we could throw firecrackers and smoke bombs a long way. And then one summer the tree was filled with cicadas and we grabbed them and held them between our fingers until they made high-pitched whines of protest. Sometimes we'd throw them and watch them fall until their wings took hold on the shimmering air and the gently curving arc of their fall turned into the equally gentle arc of their flight to some other tree or to the ground.

When they are not being manhandled—or boyhandled—they go up. If they're not flying, then they climb—up tree trunks, vines, tires, pant legs. Presented with a finger, they clutch tenaciously. Often they lose their grip, plummet to the ground, and start over again. They have been in the dark so long; now they will get as close to the sun as they can. They have been alone a long time, and now they aggressively seek one another's company. In the trees the males gather in groups to sing. Each makes clicking sounds with so-called tymbal muscles that line the hollow interior of his abdomen. The inside air resonates and amplifies those sounds, which come at a frequency of up to four hundred eighty per second. The effect has been likened to repeatedly squeezing an aluminum can. Just before the cicada begins to chirp a muscle closes his auditory organs, which are also on the abdomen. Maybe he'd go deaf otherwise. Socrates said cicadas were descended from men who, being utterly enamored of singing, neglected to eat and drink, and so died. As good a description of the effect as any I've seen comes from Donald Culross Peattie: "The sound is nothing like any intonation of the human voice, but more like the sound of a knife laid, at first lightly, on a grindstone, then pressed down hard while unyielding steel and flying stone are ground together—a cry that dies away suddenly to a dismal wail."

This dense, wall-of-sound noise of warm afternoons is an aggregating call that attracts both female and male cicadas. Females are more likely to hear and come to large groups of males. Each will fly or crawl to a singing male; if she likes what she hears and sees, the two will copulate. Several days later, she is ready to lay her eggs. She moves out toward the end of a twig (oak trees being highly regarded for this purpose), inserts a sharp rear-end organ known as an ovipositor into the wood, and digs out two small, parallel chambers. There she lays a dozen or more eggs. All told she lays four hundred to six hundred eggs, which means a great many slots cut in a great many twigs. The twigs, their flow of sap cut off, turn brown and sometimes dangle. Entomologists call this "flagging" because the leaf bunches look like brown flags waving in the wind.

After about seven weeks the eggs hatch and the young cicadas, a twelfth of an inch long, drop to the ground. Their thick forelegs are shaped something like spades, and they dig quickly into the ground, out of the reach of most predators, up to two feet down in the woodland humus. I couldn't tell you whether they go to any trouble to ensure that the spot they choose will be a good home for the next seventeen years.

◇

Cicadas are not quick, and they are subject to being eaten by a diverse range of creatures, including blackbirds, gulls, chipmunks, cats, and enterprising journalists. One biologist described their taste as "like that of a raw potato with a touch of avocado or clam juice." They are easy to catch. They furnish birds, mammals, and insects with so much food that there's no way they can all be eaten. Their sheer numbers assure the species' survival. "We do not know of a single predator that is synchronized with periodical cicadas, probably because none has been able to evolve a 17-year life cycle," wrote the entomologist Henry Dybas. "One can speculate that periodical cicadas did have synchronized predators in their early history, before the cicadas evolved their present long life cycle. If so, those cicadas that possessed the ability to delay emergence—by one year, say—would emerge above ground after their predators had come and gone, and thus they would be favored by natural selection—at least until their predators caught up. This could have initiated a contest as to which had the physiological ability to extend dormancy the longest—an evolutionary race that the cicadas won and the predators lost, with consequent extinction of the latter. This speculation may be too neat, and the hypothetical predators too conveniently disposed of, but it is hard to imagine any other plausible reason for the evolution of such an improbably long life cycle."

In the eastern United States there are three species of seventeen-year cicadas, which can be distinguished by appearance and, to some extent, by habitat: *Magicicada septendecim* likes upland woods of oak and hickory, as does the smaller *M. septendecula*; *M. cassini* prefers floodplain forests. Entomologists have classified them in "broods," according to the year of their appearance; the group I saw was Brood

XIII. Their natural history is complicated by the existence of three other types of cicadas, generally restricted to more southerly regions, that are identical in appearance to the seventeen-year varieties but emerge on a thirteen-year cycle. The relationship between the two cycles is poorly understood, but some research has suggested that seventeen-year cicadas that grow too crowded underground may accelerate their development and turn into a thirteen-year variety.

In any case, cicadas have been buzzing for a long time. Fossil cicadas have been found in sediments laid down during the Cretaceous Period, up to about a hundred and thirty-five million years ago. It's a long-running show, and that it seems wasteful or gross at times probably says more about human evolution than about how insects get by. One day I went to the botanic garden and watched a family of Canada geese—two adults and five mallard-sized goslings—make their way through a patch of underbrush. They stripped the plants of every cicada in sight, though the goslings sometimes gagged in the process of swallowing such large and leggy objects. Even more delectable, it seemed, were the empty brown husks the nymphs had shed, which crunched like pork rinds in the geese's bills.

That summer there were more red-winged blackbirds in the oaks by the beach than I'd ever seen before. Some of them had nested along the creek, and when the fledglings were old enough they went to perch and roost in the oaks. They roamed through the branches picking off cicadas right and left, setting up a racket that rivaled the insects' humming.

Late one bright afternoon I sat for a while under the arborvitae tree. The ground was littered with cicada parts—wings, legs, heads, midsections. It was a tableau of carnage. The blackbirds were fussy eaters: they picked only the choice cuts and let the rest fall. Around me I saw headless cicadas, still crawling, and upended thoraxes with legs squirming in the air. There was one cicada that lacked head and wings and abdomen and yet still crawled as if nothing was wrong. And I suppose, in a sense, nothing was. Even the chipmunks gorged themselves, leaving tidy little midden piles of body parts near their burrow entrances.

I hoped in vain to see the large wasp, *Sphecius speciosus*, the cicada-killer (which preys on several species of cicadas and so has not had to evolve a seventeen-year life cycle). Though large, they are still smaller than their prey. A female wasp will sting a cicada until the larger insect is paralyzed, making the incision with surgical precision so that the cicada is stunned but not killed. She carries the cicada to a burrow dug for the purpose and lays her eggs on it. When the eggs hatch the wasp larvae feed on their paralyzed host, eating through the cicada in a preprogrammed way that keeps it alive as long as possible. The nonessential parts are devoured first: the abdomen, the head. When, we might wonder, does the endless feeding finally wipe out whatever consciousness the cicada carries? Does it remain sentient to the very end of its own dissolution? It is dark, very dark down there, in the burrow, dark beyond our comprehension. The wasps' knowledge of cicada anatomy, their seeming embodiment of malevolence, have led more than one scientist to doubt the Darwinian theory of evolution. From what chance mutation could such cruelly specialized information have come? Ironically, the victimized cicada lives longer than the parent wasp, which dies after laying her eggs. It is somewhat comforting to suppose that the underground trance, the lying paralyzed, is perhaps not too unlike a cicada's other years underground in the nymphal burrow. Bit by bit, the body is dismantled, just the reverse of, and no worse than, the way it grew so slowly. Dust to dust, and life to life; the sun will glint, next year, on those translucent wasp wings.

As I sat under the arborvitae and watched and listened, all around me were thousands of catastrophes: cicadas crippled by unfortunate circumstance, eaten whole, dismembered, squashed underfoot unnoticed, crushed in the act of copulation by a tire. An acrid and sweetish smell loomed in the air—a scent of decay I remembered from my tenth summer. The cicadas, like the blackbirds, like all of us, were born with their clocks ticking. There were thousands, millions of individual disasters, and yet there seemed no end to the invaders. From my spot under the tree I could see, without trying, dozens of healthy, whole cicadas. And it was the same wherever I looked: they still covered branches, peonies, sidewalks. Was this what it was like when the passenger pigeons blotted out the sun for hours? Or when bison washed over tawny prairie vistas with their dark tide? In an age when nature has come to seem fragile, when it is as if our mere touch or even admiration is enough to send species careening into extinction, the cicadas rebuff our assumptions of scarcity. They live in our midst, among our millions, and they thrive. The only other creatures I'd seen in such abundance were humans, and their miseries, sufferings, and dyings were conducted mainly in private. Here it seemed the blackbirds and geese could eat until they burst, the sweet white gore and quivering legs could cover all the streets, and still the hazy air would vibrate with the frenzy of mating. The cicadas' numbers were as unimaginable to me as the carnage their arrival instigated.

No wonder, I thought, that animals in such numbers could so easily provoke a killing instinct in people. Their population was so great that it seemed nothing could diminish it. Their rank fecundity made any individual superfluous. Watching them, I could understand how in the face of the awful, wonderful flocks of pigeons and herds of bison, the only way to reassert in our own minds the authority of our individuality was to kill. We reach for the Sharps rifle, we reach for the pesticide can. We tell ourselves, for a while, that it won't have an impact on the masses, but somewhere deep down we hope it will, because otherwise what are we?

The cicadas were magnificent in their dying. Around the beginning of July a severe thunderstorm hit: a gray then black afternoon, a yellowish sky. Thunder and then the downpour wiped out the already diminishing song. The creek swelled brown and muscular, drawing into itself the gathered torrents of lawns and woods, golf course and streets. It poured into the lake, cutting a wide channel through the sand, and was churned back by the wind until it seemed there was no longer any real delineation between wave and sand, water and land.

In the evening came the preternatural clarity that can follow a storm. I walked under the dripping leaves, over the carnage left by the blackbirds, to the beach. Where the waves had reached their greatest extent on the narrow beach the damp sand was covered with a great raft of the dying. It was a ribbon perhaps two feet wide that ran the length of the beach, stretching as far as I could see to the north and south: a ribbon that in its particulars vibrated even as its outline remained roughly the same, for though many of the cicadas lay there dead, perhaps a like number still crawled and writhed. Cicadas with bedraggled wings struggled over bodies half-buried in sand. Those that had extricated themselves from the mass crawled up the drier sand higher on the beach, heading for some lonelier fate in the weedy growth of the bluff. Every time a wave rolled in, more cicadas tumbled from the chocolate water onto the sand.

That was the last day I saw cicadas in such numbers. The beach flotsam fed the mallards and gulls, and individual cicadas lingered for a few more weeks. Soon the dog-day cicadas appeared, the harvest flies, pale green and black insects that take only two years to grow to about the same size as their seventeen-year cousins; but their numbers were so much less that I could not help but think of them as dour, colorless.

With the going of the cicadas a little life went out of the summer. It was so much quieter outdoors. The red-winged blackbirds left. The chipmunks went back to eating berries. The dried leaf bundles of the oaks, dotted around the trees' crowns like carnations in a plump bouquet, presaged the colors of fall. By the time the other leaves began turning I was well ready for the change of seasons, comforted in the autumnal chill by the thought of new life already in the soil, waiting patiently for its own time in the sun, its own chance to sing its heart out.

As I looked about me I felt that the grass was the country,
as the water is the sea.
WILLA CATHER
My Ántonia

JULY: *Edges*

The arborvitae has grown smaller again, just as I had feared.
It happens every time I visit. By now I should be inured to its
diminution, but still each time I see it again I hope it will
tower with the same grandeur I remember from my boyhood.

It does not. Its trunk is not nearly as broad as I recall. Its
top reaches forty, maybe fifty feet into the air from its
gnarled base. It's not an inconsiderable tree, but when I was
a boy it was as tall and as thick around as a redwood, I swear.
When I climbed it, pulling myself up and up on its reassur-

ingly stout branches, I went so high that I thought I could almost see tomorrow, or at least the bluffs of Michigan, rising in a dark band across the lake.

I know now that if I did see anything above the lake's great blue curve it must have been clouds, or smog—a realization that does not reduce the importance that tree had for me back then.

The tree grew upward from the junction of the beach and the deep crease of the ravine, some of its roots jutting out into empty air where the creek and the lake's storm waves had eroded the clay out from under it. Its trunk was shaped like an inverted carrot, thick at the bottom and tapering gently toward the top. The bark tore off in vertical fibrous strips if you picked at it. When I was a boy the tree's most important quality was the way its smooth, horizontal branches stepped upward in regimented fashion like the rungs of a ladder. It was easy to climb. It was easy to climb all the way up to where the trunk narrowed to the thickness of a baseball bat's sweet spot. It seemed a long way up—at least, when my best friend, Eric, and I flung our firecrackers or smoke bombs toward the beach from up there it took a long time for them to reach the ground. The arborvitae was in view of the house, but while clambering among its branches we felt beyond supervision, in a world of our own.

Now it's just a tree. One of the larger ones along the shore, to be sure, but it doesn't protrude high above its neighbors, as I had remembered; it doesn't stand out. Most visitors to the beach wouldn't give it a second glance. Through the years the waves have come and gone, the creek has powered through, and it's only thanks to new bulwarks of timbers and gabions that the tree hasn't been washed into the lake's oblivion. It stands there diminished, a monument to the way time shrinks a child's wide horizons.

I shouldn't be surprised this has happened. Even when I was a child I knew it was going to, even before we moved into the big house near the clay hills. We lived half a mile farther up the shore then, and a block away from the water's edge. From the time I was very young, from a time before I can remember, my mother made a habit of taking my sisters and me to that neighborhood's beach. I cannot remember these excursions in any detail, but the accompanying sensations are among my earliest and deepest memories. They are what I suspect will be left to me when I am dying and unable to remember the names and faces of loved ones or friends, or even my own name; I believe then I will still be able to feel the cool green dimness of the ravine giving way to the glare of the beach, the prickle of coarse sand on skin, the bite of sun, the hint of cold in the lake breeze, the calls of the gulls. I believe that when I am far enough gone that time loses its meaning entirely I will recall how the sand sloped gently, almost imperceptibly, toward the blue water, and the beach stretched on forever, and there was nothing, not even the shadow of an expectation, beyond the long horizons. Behind me the slope of the wooded bluff reared up, an endless hill, with a dry cottonwood jungle at its base. Who could ever hope to see it all? How could I ever get my fill of this world?

And by the time we moved, when I was eight, those expeditions had shrunk to a mere stroll through a ravine to the beach, crowned by a small patch of woods. A good place to play, sure, but it wasn't a world anymore, not by itself. And ever since then I have known few things more intimately than the sense of loss and growth that comes from getting to know a place thoroughly and, in the process, seeing its edges, its horizons, come rushing inward. In my recollection, smoothed and gleaming as a beach pebble, the true beginnings of memory are tied less tightly to knowing something beautiful than to the understanding that it must end.

It's something of a commonplace to observe that a tree that seemed monstrous in childhood should appear merely average to an adult; that a backyard should shrink from a huge savanna to a pocket-sized patch of lawn; that the tangled jungle of a neighbor's hedge should turn into a few scraggly bushes. The scale of our surroundings changes profoundly as we grow and mature, as we come to know places more from a car than on foot or by bicycle. What I wish to examine here is less that change in itself than the way it reflects what has happened to the scale of our surrounding landscape as our culture has, for better or worse, grown and matured. And there's no better place to examine that question than the Midwest, a region whose landscape has changed so fundamentally in the last three centuries that it's a revelation to read what it was like before we applied the considerable pressures of Western civilization to it.

The first European whose descriptions of the Midwest have come down to us was Louis Joliet, who in 1673 canoed the Mississippi and Illinois Rivers. "There are prairies three, six, ten, and twenty leagues in length and three in width, surrounded by forests of the same extent," he reported to his superiors (a league is about three miles); "beyond these, the prairies begin again, so that there is as much of one sort of land as of the other."

And here is Charles Dickens, whose 1842 *American Notes* records impressions of an extensive prairie near St. Louis: "Looking towards the setting sun, there lay, stretched out before my view, a vast expanse of level ground; unbroken, save by one thin line of trees, which scarcely amounted to a scratch upon the great blank; until it met the glowing sky, wherein it seemed to dip; mingling with its rich colours, and mellowing in its distant blue. There it lay, a tranquil sea or lake without water, if such a simile be admissible, with the day going down upon it; a few birds wheeling here and there; and solitude and silence reigning paramount around."

The point is that presettlement Illinois had both woods and prairies; more important, it had *big* woods and *big* prairies. Wooded or grassy, it was a landscape of expanse and distance and silence, all of which began diminishing quickly once settlers moved in. They began to make their way into Illinois at the beginning of the nineteenth century, starting on the Ohio River and working their way up. It was like a vase slowly filling. The bottom of the vase was heavily wooded, an extension of the dense eastern forest that had stretched all the way to the Atlantic. Felling the trees for fields and pastures was a lot of work, but the place felt comfortable to the settlers—families from Kentucky, Pennsylvania, Tennessee. Higher up the vase, on the grasslands, the dearth of trees was at first thought to indicate a lack of soil fertility. It didn't take long for that falsehood to be dispelled, but even so it was easier to settle where there was lumber for houses, barns, and fences. The prairie sod was almost impossible to plow, anyway, so tightly knit together was it with the roots of drought- and fire-resistant grasses and forbs. And the open grasslands could be outright dangerous: winter blizzards raged most ferociously there, while during dry seasons fires set by lightning or by Indians could blaze for dozens of miles.

So most of the newcomers stayed in the woods, hacking down trees and planting crops, creating new fields and pastures. Then, in 1837, John Deere invented his self-cleaning steel plow in Grand Detour, Illinois. The movement onto the prairies now began in earnest. It became easier to plow an acre of prairie than it was to ax down an acre of forest. (The journalist Richard Manning wrote that the sound of the tough roots breaking for the first time "was that of a fusillade of pistols.") The settlers came and came. They planted row crops, fenced in pastures, laid out gardens. They started orchards and husbanded windbreaks where no trees had grown for centuries. On the prairie as in the forest, settlement was above all a process of creating numerous edges where various types of woodland met various types of open ground. The main job of settlement, it seemed, was to turn big patches of forest and prairie into little patches of both.

The new edges between the woods and the grassland, the settlers found, had utilitarian virtues. An edge is a transition zone that combines many of the benefits of what lies on either side. Edges are the places where you can enjoy both sun and shade, where you can plant vegetables and collect hickory nuts, collect firewood and see the stars. Edges are the places where the deer and the quail and the rabbits gather, because they too prefer the mingling of open space and shelter, as well as the rich shrubby foliage and fruit that grow where trees meet grass. Edges are opportunity and diversity. Edges are black raspberries, wild roses, apple trees, butterflies. Edges are raccoons, skunks, crows.

But the lure of edges goes deeper than practicality. In the early travelers' accounts the joy or terror of the prairie often manifests itself on first sighting, at the moment of breaking out of the dark woods into the wind and light; the aesthetic pleasure travelers find in the grasslands is greatest where scattered groves crown the hills or wind along the streambanks. The great prairie fires were fearful, but no more so than the very openness that existed in symbiosis with the flames. There was such space on the prairie, wrote Donald Culross Peattie, "that men longed for a corner, women for a neighbor." The deepest woods, too, were problematic, home to cougars, bears, imagined demons.

The lure of edges has deep psychological roots. When Walt Whitman, America's poet of grass, came west for the first time, wrote Manning, he was appalled at the openness of the plains and advocated planting trees there. It seems a practically universal trait that humans like edges and create them where they are not naturally present. Where do people most like to live? By seacoasts and lakeshores. On the banks of rivers. In forest meadows. By groves on the prairie. In the absence of natural edges, we create them: we chainsaw clearings in the woods, plant woodlots on the grassy plains, group the most prestigious addresses around urban parks and oak-shaded suburban lawns.

In the Midwest, the rest is history. The rest is a patchwork whose scale is intimate, pastoral, not grand. In creating so many edges, we have chopped the landscape into bits. A child's endless forest turns into an adult's woodlot. The vast prairies of the Prairie State turn into cornfields and pocket-sized remnants of grassland. And if the change from childhood to adulthood reflects major psychological changes, the alteration of the landscape at large has had considerable ecological corollaries. Wild animals that require large tracts of forest or grassland—bison, elk, black bears, cougars—are gone from Illinois. And many others, less charismatic, less known, are in trouble. Grassland birds like the greater prairie chicken, upland sandpiper, and northern harrier require extensive areas without trees (in which great horned owls and other predators can hide). These species have become rare in Illinois.

The same is true in forests. Wood thrushes, warblers, tanagers, vireos, and many other forest birds have been in decline throughout much of the eastern and central United States in the last few decades. The biggest culprit seems to be forest fragmentation. When forests are cut into smaller pieces, predators that thrive along edges—raccoons, crows, blue jays, rat snakes—expand their ranges. They devour birds' eggs.

Brown-headed cowbirds like edges, too. Cowbirds don't build nests of their own; rather, they lay their eggs in the nests of other birds. Their eggs hatch quickly, and their chicks are aggressive, so that the foster parents often end up raising baby cowbirds rather than their own baby thrushes or warblers. Cowbirds are a species of open country, but with the opening of forest habitat they can find the nests of many forest species that did not evolve in conjunction with cowbirds. Research in southern Illinois's Shawnee National Forest has shown that even wood thrush nests over 300 meters from the edge of large forest patches had a better than 90 percent likelihood of being discovered and parasitized by cowbirds. The islands of forest there—among the largest left in the state—are growing too small for wood thrushes. The species presumably survives in the area only because enough surplus birds are raised in other larger forest areas to spill over into the Shawnee. If those other islands suffer the same fate, the wood thrush's sweet, ethereal song may soon become vanishingly scarce in Illinois.

I would argue that there are psychological corollaries to this change, too, changes perhaps as profound as the difference between a child's and an adult's perception of one's surroundings. With the passing of the prairie's spaces, as with the disappearance of the silence of the deep woods, we have lost something. Call it a sense of possibility. Call it innocence. The large scale and the fearful openness the early travelers found in the long prairie vistas are gone. And so is the glory.

It's the Fourth of July, and Eric and I are high in the arborvitae, launching fusillades of bottle rockets and smoke bombs. We are as pyromaniacal as any nine-year-old boys, and we have stockpiled our weapons and planned the day as methodically as though it were a true military campaign. The fun lasts all day, from shooting off the first firecrackers in the morning to swimming in the afternoon and finishing off with brilliant roman candles at night, waiting in the quiet dusk for the hushed hiss as each missile hits the water. We're littering, we're making a mess, and we're having a swell time. There's room all around us to make noise, to romp—woods and beach—and there's the sweet and spacious feeling too of having virtually the entire summer stretch out before us, the span of two months seeming so long at that age that the knowledge of school cranking up again at its end is no more than a vague notion, a quiet hint, easy to overlook entirely. At age nine we've just learned some swear words and so we can say, "To hell with school. Let's have fun."

That innocence washed off some time ago. The beach and the tree have shrunk; the creek is a muddy ditch. But whenever I return to the shore I try to grasp some of what filled me then. I grab a handful of sand and feel how its wet coarseness leaves my hands raw and red. Or I look out at the porcelain perfection of the lake on a sunny day, a scene that looks precisely the same now as then. It's the one horizon I can look at that hasn't changed, the single place that manifests no loss. At lake's edge it is still possible to gain that sense of spacious possibility that the early prairie travelers wrote of: possibility, and a bit of fear.

Look: the lake is sunlight captured and given liquid form. Far from shore its deep water is rich cerulean. Closer in it glows azure, turquoise, lazuli. Brownish patches show where sandbars rise near the surface. When the wind blows from the north or east the waves rise and churn brown clouds of sand and silt from the bottom. The wind comes in strong and clear from over the lake and the whitecaps are icing on the cake, a gratuity. The gulls, bobbing and screaming, are the lake incarnate, pure white distillation of fish and mussels and the cast-up dead. And for a moment, just for a moment, the horizon goes on forever.

For the one essential quality of a wave is that it moves;
anything that retards or stops its motion dooms it to dissolution
and death.

RACHEL CARSON
The Sea around Us

AUGUST: *Waves*

It doesn't take much to get a wave going on the lake, not
much at all—just a slight dimple from any old breath of air,
which the wind enlarges and turns into a ripple, then a slight
ridge that in turn catches more wind, and already you've got
a wave, then a series of waves. You've got yourself, as sailors
say, a sea. If the wind keeps blowing from the same direction
its waves grow until the slope of the water becomes too great
to be maintained, at which point the waves tumble forward
in a welter of foam and spray: whitecaps.

I can't remember a time when I didn't have waves going through my head, the echoing rhythm of waves hitting the shore, any shore, somewhere. It's as if I'm always standing near the beach on a stormy day when the surf is booming. The sand is stretched tight as a drum and it resonates as if the waters were running beneath it. That's the aural backdrop in my head, the white noise I've grown used to. Doesn't matter where I am. You might say waves are my first language, not only what I always hear in my inner ear but also the filter through which I perceive the world. Everything I hear echoes their endless cycle. When I stop to listen, my breaths hiss gently like big combers that rise slowly, break, and fade into a sighing foam. Now the snow is falling and the light is slowly rising through the gray morning; now the afternoon sun slaps the rocks of a desert mountain wall; now a flock of grackles flies by in sinuous motion; and to me all these things are echoes of that first deep rhythm, a foaming and churning of sound that falls into silence and rises again. This is intimate; this remains.

Maybe everyone carries some such rhythm around with them, as the Hopis both shape and are shaped by the pulsing beat of their endless dances, the drumming and chanting that even the unborn babies have heard for so long, already, that they will not forget it their entire lives. I credit this particular rhythm to my mother's taking me to the beach when I couldn't even walk yet, or maybe to living within earshot of the lake longer than I can remember. Or maybe it's because I was born in a hospital within sight of the lake. I don't know where it comes from, and really it doesn't matter. In any case I always find myself drawn to water, on city beaches, in the suburbs, on visits to the ocean shore, on cool fall days. I am pulled to any old body of water like a tern, a heron, a duck.

Part of the lure of the water is the talk of sailors, which has its own peculiar, archaic rhythm. A *swell*: the proper and precise term for a wave on the open lake. A *sea*: not only a body of water, but more specifically a stormy one, a collection of waves. A *fetch*: the extent of water across which a wind can blow, raising waves. On Lake Michigan a north-northeaster can play across a fetch of some three hundred miles before its waves thunder onto the narrow Illinois beaches—a trivial distance, perhaps, compared to the fetches of thousands of miles on the open ocean, but enough to raise waves ten to fifteen feet high that astonish visitors who have never seen the Great Lakes before.

When such a surf hits the shore the force of its water is obvious—the waves crash down and forward, running up the sand, lapping at the feet of bluffs or apartment buildings—but only when a wave enters shallow water do its constituent molecules actually move in this horizontal manner. Out on the open lake each water molecule moves up and down in a roughly circular motion, borrowed first by one wave, then another, and another, in an endless succession, always returning more or less to the place it began. It's a good thing; otherwise a northeast wind, say, could blow much of the lake's water onto the southwest shore. A wave is not a thing discrete but rather a rhythm, an interaction, a sympathy.

No doubt it is partly this property of waves, that they embody ceaseless motion and stasis at the same time, that makes watching and listening to them such a profoundly meditative occupation. The eye lingers on the waves crowding in one after the other, in unending rhythm; theirs is the ineluctable pull of a place that is not ours and that will look just the same after we are gone. On the lake the wakes of boats vanish in a gust of wind and piers are knocked down in a few decades. On the beach we see the broadest of horizons. Going there, we can look as far outside ourselves as this world ever allows.

A few summers ago the lake turned green. The several hundred feet of water nearest the shore glowed rich emerald, a vivid, unhealthy-looking color. A swimmer rising from the water was liable to emerge looking like a B-movie monster, covered from head to toe with specks and strands of livid algae.

When I looked closely, through a hand lens, each algal strand turned out to be composed of a lengthy series of individual cells, strung together single file like a trainload of coal cars. Each cell was cylindrical and filled with clear protoplasm, and in each hung suspended a long, spiral chloroplast, the translucent green body that houses the alga's chlorophyll—its photosynthetic powerhouse. I called an aquatic biologist, Ellen Marsden of the Illinois Natural History Survey, and she gave me the plant's name: spirogyra.

A spirogyra cell can survive on its own, I learned, but they tend to live in long strands. Perhaps they have a better chance of withstanding the turbulence of storm waves without being cast ashore than do single cells. In any case, green algae of this sort have been bobbing and multiplying in waves for a long, long time; the fossils of similar filamentous algae have been found in rocks from the Precambrian era, which ended some 600 million years ago.

Marsden speculated that zebra mussels were behind the great algal bloom. Zebra mussels, as boaters and public-utility workers know, are native to Eurasia, but were discovered in the Great Lakes in the late 1980s. Their arrival is one of the ironies of the movement to clean up the environment. Oceangoing freighters once carried oil as ballast, and dumped it into harbors when taking on cargo. Since that practice was banned with the passage of the Clean Water Act, water has been used as ballast instead. Water from a foreign port may not pollute immediately, like oil, but now each ship has the potential of delivering a healthy and insidious load of some exotic new species to the Great Lakes—and an invasive species can be far more devastating in the long run than any oil spill.

It's believed that water containing juvenile, free-swimming zebra mussels was scooped up by a freighter in the Black Sea around 1986 and released in the St. Clair River, the waterway that connects Lakes Huron and Erie. Since then, their population has exploded throughout the Great Lakes and other inland waterways. Prolific breeders, the mussels clog power plant input pipes, foul the hulls of boats and ships, and suffocate bottom-dwelling native fauna like the colorful and endangered Higgins eye and winged mapleleaf mussels.

Zebra mussels feed by filtering particles from the water; they digest the edible bits and eject the rest onto the lake bottom. A lot of mussels need a lot of food. Each mussel filters and clarifies something like a quart of water per day. In the summer of 1992 measurements showed that the lake was clearer than at any time in recent decades. Sunlight could penetrate farther below the surface than previously, and algae thrived, enjoying for a while their own uncontrolled population boom.

For me, the green water was a mental challenge, and not just because I wanted to swim on hot August afternoons. It was a challenge because I derive deep comfort from the idea that the lake does not change. The wind still plays across its waters as it did when the glacier that formed it melted, when the first Indian paddled a rough canoe along its shore, or when Jean Nicolet put ashore in Green Bay in the seventeenth century, wearing his best ceremonial robes because he thought he had arrived in the Orient. The lake sinks ships, devours beaches, floods Lake Shore Drive. Our inability to control it may fool us into thinking it a wilderness that changes only at its own pace.

But this reassuring thought is only an illusion. In fact the lake's ecology has been altered more profoundly even than that of the surrounding forests and prairies and marshes that have erupted into the concrete and lawns of our cities and suburbs. The lake once teemed with giant sturgeon and lake trout, whitefish and emerald shiners—all of them now gone or much reduced in numbers. Now its most abundant residents are alewives and coho salmon, smelt and zebra mussels—species introduced deliberately or accidentally by humans.

Often the newcomers interact in unexpected ways. In 1990 scientists found two more inadvertent imports from the Old World in the St. Clair River—tubenose and round gobies. Ironically, both species seem to like feeding on zebra mussels. Given time, they may establish an equilibrium with the bivalves. But their effects on other species are unknown; already biologists have noted that the mottled sculpin, a small native fish, has disappeared from areas where the gobies have become common.

A few years ago Ellen Marsden estimated that there were about 180 introduced species living in the Great Lakes. "We're really in kind of a mess right now," she told me. "As a pure scientist it's fascinating, because you get to watch being tested for you all the theories about invasion biology and ecological stability and how species respond to perturbations. As an applied biologist, a lot of the work one does is aiding managers in keeping systems stable so that we can make use of them without destroying them. From that standpoint, it makes you want to weep. It is so hard to predict the effect of these exotic species."

During the summer of the green water I engaged in my own dabblings in practical ecology. Whenever I went for a walk in the local forest preserves I pulled up a few stalks of garlic mustard, an invasive plant from Eurasia that has spread widely in the woodlands and forests of the northern Midwest. It is a distinctive plant with heart-shaped leaves and a fetid odor, as you'd guess from the name. In late spring it sets out modest spires of small, cross-shaped white flowers. By summer the flowers turn into long, pointed seedpods and the dying plants slowly turn a tawny yellow. By midsummer, in many well-shaded midwestern woodlands, these upright spikes are the dominant vegetation under the canopy of trees and shrubs.

Garlic mustard seeds prolifically and sprouts early in the spring, shading out many other woodland plants. A biennial, it spends its first year growing a low, inconspicuous rosette of leaves and storing food in its roots. In its second year it shoots up its flowering stalk, which when pollinated results in abundant seeds. Deer, and apparently other herbivores as well, do not like garlic mustard and will eat it only in extremity, preferring the native wildflowers—which are additionally in decline because the alien biennial has shaded them out of many areas.

When I tugged, the shallow root systems of the invader came free easily. I'd gather a heaping armful at the beginning of a walk and feel that I was paying a sort of toll for enjoying the woods. It was enjoyable work, a good excuse for roaming, even though there was so much of the stuff that when I stopped to think about the effort in practical terms I knew I was probably wasting my time: the disturbed ground I left behind was an ideal seedbed for a new generation of garlic mustard plants.

Nonetheless, it was deeply satisfying to pull the plants up. Even the large, branched specimens came up so easily that I found myself thinking, *Anything so shallow-rooted does not belong here.* I found myself looking more closely at the forest floor than ever before, noticing the low white clusters of wild leek flowers, the rare orange splash of a slime mold on a rotting log.

In rich soil, in shade, the garlic mustard grew three feet high. In more open areas with poor soil the work was harder because the plants were stunted and I had to stoop to pull them. Many of the stems were only a few inches high, with only a few small leaves; yet even these had produced one or two full-sized seedpods. Like a single mother working two jobs to put her kids through college, they were throwing everything into providing for the future.

I pulled and yanked, but the more garlic mustard I removed, the more I saw. You might call it the naturalist's paradox: we may be driven by the positive forces of love, curiosity, or fascination, but the more closely we look at our environment the more we become aware of the often deleterious effect our actions have on other animals and plants. We come to see how the landscape has been altered by our actions, including the countless living changes we have wrought on the landscape: house sparrows and dandelions, starlings and Norway rats, zebra mussels and garlic mustard, all relative newcomers, along with most of us, on this continent, all opportunists and generalists— again, like us—that tend to outcompete native species, at least in the short term. It is difficult to find any place in North America, however remote, that does not support some invasive, nonnative species. Without concerted control efforts, these opportunistic plants and animals may wipe out many native species that have evolved over thousands or millions of years in conjunction with particular places. The result would be a homogenization of the world's ecology, closely paralleling the homogenization of the world's human culture that is proceeding at an astounding rate today thanks to television and other Western influences. We are an adaptable species, and I have no doubt that people can survive in a world of zebra mussels and garlic mustard and *Seinfeld*, but I'd prefer to live where the yellow lady's-slippers and Higgins eye mussels—and indigenous dancing and music and food and religious beliefs—can still be found. Diversity—natural and cultural—is a gift of life that should not be carelessly discarded.

We have to be realistic about this. There is no turning back the clock. We can't wipe out alien species any more than we can get rid of TV. Indeed, how could we do so without sending a whole lot of Americans back overseas? But we should do all we can to make sure the natives have a chance to persist in health into the future. The very least we can do is this: go into the woods, or the prairies, and make sure all the plants and animals that live there now can survive over the long term. Our grandchildren deserve no less than the chance to see them. And as residents that have been here longer than we have, native species have a right to exist that is all their own.

One of the greatest virtues of restoring ecosystems so that native species can persist is that it is a hopeful act. Nowhere has this hope been expressed more profoundly than in the forest preserves around Chicago, where since the 1970s a dedicated and growing corps of volunteers has been working to restore the prairies and airy oak savannas that had grown into thick woods depauperate in native species. By cutting back and burning invasive species and planting seeds of native grasses and forbs, these activists have been able to reconstruct ecosystems that were almost lost. At a time when it seems the human presence in the landscape is often portrayed as being relentlessly detrimental to most plants and animals, this work is both a manifestation of hope for the future and an expression of confidence that human beings can play a positive role in promoting biodiversity.

Which is why, when I tired of pulling garlic mustard, I began to collect seeds of some of the native woodland plants. My parents would be moving soon and I wanted to give them some native seeds for their new yard. I walked the ravine behind the old house searching out the bristling stalks of bottlebrush grass, the sticky seedpods of tick-trefoils, and the wiry, slender stems of woodland brome grass. One hot day I found a patch of woodland brome along the path by the sluggish creek. Its heads dangled heavy-seeded, turning a crisp, light brown, while its stems still retained shades of yellow and green. It was easy to harvest the seeds by running my right hand up the stems; the ripe seeds fell off easily into my left hand, whereas the unripe seeds clung tightly. I decided to be sloppy, letting many of the seeds fall to the ground for the chipmunks, for the wind, for the next spring.

As my collecting envelope slowly filled I thought, *This is like the beginning of agriculture.* I imagined people bending under loaded baskets, saving the seeds from those plants that bore most heavily, saying, *Let us save these for planting in the spring.* It seemed amazing that the moist and rounded earth, so rich with the smells of decay, could produce something so dry, so perfect and ascetic, as these stalks of seeds dangling in balanced grace.

I left the seeds in my parents' freezer, then planted them behind their new house the next spring. I didn't wash the dirt out from under my fingernails for a long time.

I was squeamish about the green water, but still I went swimming later that afternoon. I'd learned about the algae and their antiquity by then, and I felt I was stepping into an organic broth, a fountainhead of life like that from which organisms first emerged from water onto dry land hundreds of millions of years ago. I imagined trilobites and cephalopods lurking on the unseen bottom.

The sun was hot, and the water almost tropical by Lake Michigan standards—65 degrees or so. A cooling southeast wind was freshening; serried, choppy waves were rising to the height of a foot or two. As always, I gasped involuntarily from the cold. The bottom consisted mainly of rounded cobbles that were painful to walk on, and it was a relief to finally get out to where the water was chest deep, where I could float free. I swam parallel to the shore, heading first north along the beach, then south, occasionally getting a noseful of lake water when a wave topped out a little higher than the others. When I felt tired I turned over onto my back and let myself drift with the swells.

Above me a gull hung motionless on the breeze. It faced southeast for ten seconds or more, poised on slender wings, then turned its head slightly to the right. It cut its wings to a sharper angle and drifted to the right a little, slowly at first then faster and faster, finally disappearing behind the trees, flying as swiftly as a falcon.

I breathed slowly, pushing my arms down every ten seconds or so to help keep myself afloat. It was an almost effortless motion and I found myself thinking, *This is the only way I can know what the birds know, this floating and drifting on waves.* Wind must feel something like water as it holds a body aloft.

I plunged my arms down into the limpid water, and silver streamers of bubbles trailed from my fingers. I tried to imagine waves as they must look from high above, how they form long lines that stitch the lake's surface together, disappearing over the horizon, beyond the limits of sight, until a new wind arises and forms new waves that run in a contrary direction and wipe out the old ones. The view ran back through time; I tried to imagine how the lake appeared to the first bird that ever hovered above its waters on a stiff breeze.

Plants and animals and people, I was thinking, pass through places like waves. Every species that evolved in or was brought to North America has spread out from its point of origin in widening circles. The green algae have been casting their tendrils on inland waters since before North America was separated from the other continents. The gulls have been around for millions of years. The first human wave began some tens of thousands of years ago in what is now Alaska. Long after its ripples spread over all the land that was available and achieved a certain equilibrium, it was swamped by a new wave from Europe and Africa and Asia that sloshed messily over much of the continent and continues to spread: through the Sunbelt, through the Northwest, pooling heavily on the prairies now being turned into dense subdivisions. The zebra mussel wave began only recently but since then has rippled throughout the Great Lakes and now laps on the convoluted and muddy shores of the Mississippi and its myriad tributaries. The fortunes of other creatures, spirogyra or sturgeon or the Higgins eye mussel, rise and fall in sympathetic vibration, and if some drop out of the cycle entirely, there are others ready to take their places.

Everything scientists have learned about ecology has taught us that we do not, and probably cannot, know all the effects of these ecological waves. Even the dirt of the well-trodden Cook County forest preserves is chock-full of bacteria, insects, and other organisms that have never been named or described. We don't know what role they play in the system. We don't know what the spread of garlic mustard does to them. The more we learn about ecology, the more we realize that we are adrift in a sea of organisms that coexist in patterns of almost unbelievable complexity. What we do learn to comprehend, when we are honest with ourselves, is the depth of our ignorance.

And what is it we should do with our ignorance? Maybe this: swim, get dirt under our fingernails, raise children well, try to ensure they have at least as many opportunities as we did. We cannot know where any of these ripples will end up. But what we can know, perhaps all too rarely, is this: the fluid grace that lies in swimming, in the churning of the waves, in the measured pace of a walk through the woods, in the breath we exhale into the cool lake breeze.

The passenger pigeon needs no protection. Wonderfully prolific, having the vast forests of the North as its breeding grounds, traveling hundreds of miles in search of food, it is here to-day, and elsewhere to-morrow, and no ordinary destruction can lessen them, or be missed from the myriads that are yearly produced.

COMMITTEE REPORT TO OHIO STATE LEGISLATURE, 1857

SEPTEMBER: *Pigeons*

By September the summer sounds of the forest preserve had mainly died away. The dog-day cicadas still hummed incessantly, but among the birds only the crows and the blue jays with their aggressive *hee-yer! hee-yer!* bothered calling much during the last lingering afternoons of summer. The birds that enlivened the woods with their songs during the breeding season were quiet now. They existed only as faint rustlings hidden behind the leaves, tiny chirps or flits of wings half heard.

Along the railroad tracks the ashes and cottonwoods were turning yellow, the sumacs and Virginia creepers twining the trunks with brilliant crimson. Their shadows grew long in the afternoon, presaging the chill of fall. The leaves had done most of their photosynthetic work already, the birds had nested and raised their young, the insects had spun their cocoons and hidden their eggs in the crevices and holes the chickadees and woodpeckers would probe all winter long, and it seemed as though the whole world was just waiting for the days to get shorter and colder.

Among the trees the air pooled still and warm, though above me I could see the wind swaying the high crowns of the white oak trees. Among their leaves, still glossy green, I could see the abundant, small round shapes of acorns, and once in a while I heard one drop into the leaf litter, sheared off by wind or, more likely, the toothwork of a chipmunk or gray squirrel. I wished I'd brought my hat; being hit by an acorn falling fifty feet is an unfortunately memorable experience.

White oaks are a masting species, producing large crops of acorns in some years and very few in others. Generally all the trees in a given area are on the same schedule. It takes a lot of energy to produce a lot of seeds, so oaks store food for a few years and then go all out. As many as eight or nine years of scarcity, or more commonly three to five, may pass between masting years. The trees then produce so many acorns—up to seven thousand on a single large tree—that all the woods' blue jays, red-headed woodpeckers, squirrels, chipmunks, and deer together cannot eat them all. Some fall unnoticed among the leaf litter. Others are buried and forgotten by jays and squirrels, which carry the seeds farther from their parent trees than the wind could ever do. Next spring's rains will pull from the ground a bumper crop of oak seedlings. The acorns will also produce a brief but noticeable surge in the populations of squirrels, jays, and chipmunks.

The lives of those animals are so intertwined with those of the oaks that it's as if they all composed one great organism. The system by which oaks reproduce and feed their attendant animals seems so well oiled that it is easy to forget how radically different it once was. Only a little over a century ago the primary consumer of acorns was the passenger pigeon, and a walk in the oak woods likely was a profoundly different experience.

There is much talk these days of endangered species. Politicians and developers complain of the expense, and the red tape, of protecting them; conservationists hold up the specter of extinction as a haunting reminder of what our great-grandchildren may remember about us—that we were too greedy, or too careless, to protect a legacy that belongs to the ages. I go to the woods in part for refuge from this debate, and also because I want to know what it means when an animal becomes extinct. Americans of my great-grandparents' generation knew the pigeons. What marks has this most famous symbol of extinction in North America left us? And so each time I walk in the woods I listen hard for what has been lost and wonder whether the silence that yearly pervades the woods is not something created rather than the inherent voice of the season.

The passenger pigeon winged its way into Western history on July 1, 1534, when Jacques Cartier, nosing along the coast of Prince Edward Island, saw what he called an "infinite number" of the birds flying by. That is roughly what Americans were to see for the next three and a half centuries; by the time they realized that the pigeon populations were in fact not infinite, never had been, never could be, it was too late to save them. The passenger pigeons were neither the first nor the only "inexhaustible" resource to be decimated in North America— think of the great auk, the Atlantic right whale, the bison, the old-growth hardwood forests of the Ohio Valley, the towering white pines of the North Woods—but their disappearance made the greatest impression on the greatest number of people. For several generations, as settlers moved into the eastern deciduous forests, the pigeons were not just part of their lives, but the most stunning of all the biological spectacles on a continent rife with wonders.

A passenger pigeon was slightly larger than a mourning dove and had the same sort of long, delicately tapered tail we see today on the smaller bird. A female pigeon looked much like a large dove. The male was resplendent, with a back of azure and a breast of ruddy red-orange. Especially around its head and neck, some of its feathers sported a surface iridescence. When Edward B. Clark saw a male illuminated by the sunrise in Lincoln Park in April 1894—one of the last seen in the wild anywhere by a reliable observer, and probably the very last seen within Chicago's city limits—he reported that "every feather shone, and the bird's neck was gem-like in its brilliancy."

In earlier years no one bothered about single passenger pigeons. No hunter set out to shoot an individual pigeon; the goal was hundreds, or thousands. Naturalists wrote of massive, unbelievable flocks. Early in the nineteenth century the ornithologist Alexander Wilson saw a flight of pigeons over a mile wide and several birds deep that passed overhead for four hours in Kentucky. "They were flying, with great steadiness and rapidity, at a height beyond gunshot, in several strata deep, and so close together, that, could shot have reached them, one discharge could not have failed of bringing down several individuals," he wrote. "From right to left, far as the eye could reach, the breadth of this vast procession extended, seeming every where equally crowded."

Wilson conservatively estimated that the flock held over 2.2 billion birds. Another flight of pigeons seen crossing into Ontario from the United States was estimated at 3.7 billion. John James Audubon reported watching a stream of pigeons fly overhead for three days. As much as 40 percent of the bird population of the contiguous United States may have consisted of passenger pigeons.

Strong fliers, they were found from the Gulf Coast to the boreal forests of Ontario and Quebec; their scientific name, *Ectopistes migratorius*, means "migratory wanderer." They could cover hundreds of miles a day, descending periodically upon tracts of hardwood forest to gorge on acorns and beechnuts. They settled in such numbers that limbs and even entire large trees broke, killing hundreds of birds as they hit the ground. Their dung soon covered the ground like snow and killed all the underbrush. Where they had roosted the forests were wrecked—trees dead or dying, shrubs suffocated, nuts all gone. Pioneers were grateful because a pigeon visit could make the work of clearing the forest easier. They were, in Aldo Leopold's neat phrase, "a biological storm."

"When alighted, they are seen industriously throwing up the withered leaves in quest of the fallen mast," wrote Audubon. "The rear ranks are continually rising, passing over the main body, and alighting in front, in such rapid succession, that the whole flock seems still on the wing. The quantity of ground thus swept is astonishing, and so completely has it been cleared, that the gleaner who might follow in their rear would find his labor completely lost. Whilst feeding, their avidity is at times so great that in attempting to swallow a large acorn or nut, they are seen gasping for a long while, as if in agonies of suffocation.

"On such occasions, when the woods are filled with these pigeons, they are killed in immense numbers, although no apparent diminution ensues."

Their nestings were more spectacular still. Hundreds of millions, perhaps billions, of pigeons nested together, in long swaths that stretched several miles wide and dozens of miles long. When the pigeons nested north of Petoskey, Michigan, in 1878 (by which time their numbers were already on the decline), their nests were distributed over an area estimated at one hundred thousand acres—a stretch of forest forty miles long and two to three miles wide.

The largest trees held over a hundred flimsy nests, built in every favorable crotch. The noise was terrific. Wilson spoke to local people who had hunted at a great nesting: "Several of them informed me, that the noise in the woods was so great as to terrify their horses, and that it was difficult for one person to hear another speak, without bawling in his ear," he reported. "The ground was strewed with broken limbs of trees, eggs, and young squab pigeons, which had been precipitated from above, and on which herds of hogs were fattening. Hawks, buzzards, and eagles were sailing about in great numbers and seizing the squabs from their nests at pleasure; while, from twenty feet upwards to the tops of the trees, the view through the woods presented a perpetual tumult of crowding and fluttering multitudes of pigeons, their wings roaring like thunder, mingled with the frequent crash of falling timber; for now the axe-men were at work, cutting down those trees that seemed to be most crowded with nests, and contrived to fell them in such a manner, that, in their descent, they might bring down several others; by which means the falling of one large tree sometimes produced two hundred squabs, little inferior in size to the old ones, and almost one mass of fat. . . . It was dangerous to walk under these flying and fluttering millions, from the frequent fall of large branches, broken down by the weight of the multitudes above, and which, in their descent, often destroyed numbers of the birds themselves; while the clothes of those engaged in traversing the woods were completely covered with the excrements of the pigeons."

Once the telegraph and railroad arrived, news of nestings spread fast and people traveled from distant states to take advantage. Adult pigeons were shot or baited with wheat soaked in whiskey. They were suffocated by smoke from fires lit on the forest floor. Hundreds were trapped at one time with nets set up at the salt licks they liked to frequent, lured there by captive pigeons set on perches known as stools—the origin of the term *stool pigeon*. Flightless young were knocked out of their nests with long poles. Where pigeons nested in birch trees, the bark was lit afire and the young collected when they jumped from their nests to avoid the flames. The squabs hit the ground like ripe apples, so fat sometimes that they burst open as they landed. Wagons piled high with pigeons trailed away from the nestings. "Pigeons become the order of the day at dinner, breakfast, and supper," wrote Wilson, "until the very name becomes sickening."

Pigeons were taken both for immediate local consumption and for shipment to metropolitan markets. As late as 1880 a dozen cleaned adult pigeons could be bought for about $1.50 in Chicago; squabs were a trifle more expensive. It was possible to trap thousands of pigeons a day near a large nesting. Trappers could make $500 during four weeks of nesting—enough money that there was no need to work for the rest of the year. It's no wonder that when voices were raised against the slaughter, and even when laws were passed prohibiting the taking of pigeons in or near nesting areas, they were almost universally ignored.

Audubon commented on this style of hunting: "Persons unacquainted with these birds might naturally conclude that such dreadful havoc would soon put an end to the species. But I have satisfied myself, by long observation, that nothing but the gradual diminution of our forests can accomplish their decrease." He may have been right. Though millions might be killed at a large nesting, billions were left. It's likely that the disruption of nesting areas—many pigeons abandoned their nests once the shooting or burning started—had a much greater effect than outright killing. And the "diminution of our forests" probably had the greatest impact. As the great eastern forest was cleared for fields the pigeons simply had fewer and fewer places where they could fill up on acorns and beechnuts. The committee that reported to the Ohio legislature in 1857 had this right in recommending against hunting restrictions; "no ordinary destruction" could diminish the pigeons. What occurred, instead, was an extraordinary destruction of the birds' habitat that could not help but end in their demise.

The decline came so quickly that many observers suggested the birds had migrated en masse to South America or drowned in the Gulf of Mexico. Huge nestings occurred through the 1870s. By the mid-1890s, sightings of even single pigeons had become rare. The last individual in captivity, named Martha, died in Cincinnati in 1914, having lived in a cage alone for the last five years of her life as the final representative of a species already extinct.

Though their life history was never well studied, ornithologists now believe that passenger pigeons were so socially inclined that they were stimulated to breed only when a certain critical mass of other pigeons was present—a thousand, ten thousand; nobody knows how many were needed. We might imagine that small flocks of pigeons should have been able to survive, descending like breezes rather than storms on the oaks, as do flocks of hungry jays; but they were not such a species. They needed one another. They needed *many* of one another. A pair of pigeons, male and female, was not a biologically functioning unit unless surrounded by many, many others. They were absolutely incapable of living life on a small scale.

⌀

At the Burpee Museum of Natural History in Rockford, Illinois, you can see a pair of passenger pigeons ranked in a glass case with the ducks and warblers and hawks and other local birds. They are dusty stuffed birds, not the least bit lifelike. Some of the glittering iridescence remains on the male's neck, though, and in the bulge of the wing muscles and the sweep of the tails you can get a vague sense of what it would have been like to have a flight of these birds wing swiftly overhead. Even a single pair of these birds, as they swerved toward extinction, would have been noticeable.

I can imagine, having seen what these two have become, how the man who shot them—it almost certainly was a man, in those days—felt justified in doing so. In the days before the Endangered Species Act, the top priority often was *killing*, not saving, the last individuals of a species, for museum specimens, or to confirm a sighting. I can imagine how the pigeons flew in, one last time, just two this time instead of the multitudes, but still they flew quickly in out of nowhere, strong fliers, and the sun reflected in many colors from the male's neck. Had the gunner not shot, that vision of passing beauty would have been gone forever, never to return; and so he shot, more out of love than greed, and met his mark, and the birds fell. And though the lifeless bodies lost their luster, they were at least a slight reminder of what had been. I think of those pigeons spiraling downward whenever I see a bird or butterfly or flower that is so beautiful that I want to hold on to it for good. And although I know—I *know*—that the moment cannot be preserved, because it contains the frangible beauty of things that pass, sometimes I pick the flower, or try to catch the butterfly by its wings, and later when I look at it again it is my sorrow that merely hints at what I saw before.

⌀

From a car, the forest preserve flashes by in less than a minute. Inside the woods the noise of the local roads, and of the highway a mile away, is never out of earshot. Yet imagine how the place appears to one of the chipmunks gathering acorns for winter storage. A chipmunk could be born, live, and die within the few acres of the preserve, never having to cross a road, never even seeing a car. When the acorn crop fails, it makes no difference to that chipmunk whether the nuts are abundant a few miles to the west or north. Those places are not part of its world.

The pigeons comprehended the landscape in a different way. To them the entire eastern forest that stretched from the Gulf Coast to Hudson Bay was of a piece. It was all home. In spring the great flocks flew north as far as they had to until they found areas with enough acorns or beechnuts left from the previous fall to support a month of nesting. Afterward they flew farther north, or east, or west, always in search of big trees for roosting, nuts for food. They were birds of passage. They lived on a continental scale. And in the amount of food they ate, and in the amount of waste they deposited, and in the way they could destroy thousands of acres of forest by their mere presence, they were among the rarest of animals: those that could alter the landscape on the same scale as could humans.

The pigeons shared this quality with the bison of the plains that traveled by the millions, grazing prairies to stubble, then moving on. There was simply no way these animals could coexist with modern Americans, not in their wild form. As North America was settled its new people took on a lifestyle oddly similar to that of the pigeons. We didn't eat the acorns or the grass, not directly, but our hogs and cattle did. We moved in, cut the trees, plowed the prairie, hunted out the game, and always we could move on to virgin lands elsewhere. We were nomadic, restless. Always there was more forest, more grass, more game, more pure water—out west, up north, somewhere. As a few voices began to protest against the slaughter, this was the refrain in the second half of the nineteenth century: There will always be more pigeons. There is infinite room for them to nest in the north, or in the west. They have flown to South America. There are too many for us to wipe them all out. Our hunting can make no difference. As late as the 1950s some still claimed the pigeons would turn up somewhere.

Voices questioning the killing spoke out while the birds were still abundant, in the 1870s and earlier, but even then they came far too late. There was no way for us to avoid wiping them out; we could have done so only by changing the way we live. Their demise was inevitable once the Puritans set foot on what they termed a "waste and howling wilderness" that needed to be conquered, subjugated, its forests leveled, its prairie sod overturned. We had to get rid of them because they competed with us in shaping the landscape. There was no way we could have set up preserves for them, because the oaks and beeches masted in different places every year, and so the pigeons nested and fed somewhere new every year. We could not have preserved enough habitat for them without converting our American civilization into something more closely resembling the way the natives lived, in low densities that did not require the clearing of much forest or the breaking of much prairie. We would have had to adapt ourselves to the land, instead of the other way around. Human life can exist comfortably on such a small scale, but Western civilization as we know it cannot. Shopping malls, tollways, and the vast corn and soybean fields of the Midwest exist only because there is a large population that wants or needs them. When we met the passenger pigeons, it was like the waves of two great storms meeting in mid-ocean: they crisscross for a while, but given enough time the more powerful one cancels out the other.

But some ripples do remain, spreading out through the centuries and millennia. When the wind blows in September the largest of the white oaks continue to wave their uppermost twigs free and clear, tracing delicate and transitory patterns on the sky. Some are two to three feet in diameter; they may be over a century old. Maybe they were saplings when the pigeons stormed in and filled the branches of the larger trees overhead, or moved like a living carpet of brown and blue and ruddy orange over the leaf litter. Maybe one year the chipmunks starved because the pigeons ate all the acorns. Maybe the ancestors of the jays whose calls pierce the warm air had to fly miles to feed after the swarm descended. Maybe the undeniable fecundity of the rich black soil that shows here and there below the litter of fallen leaves is still attributable in small part to the drifts of pigeon droppings working their way through the endless cycling of growth and decay, plant and animal, life and death. Certainly the unceasing sound of cars and trucks on the highway, a mile west, says more than any words about the restless striving and the will to build, the need to subjugate the land to our desires, that wiped the pigeons out.

I don't go to the woods to grieve about something I can't change, but rather to sense the bare earth of reality, a richness that exists in counterpoint to what has been lost. And so at the end of the summer, when acorns ripen, I listen for the ghost of wings beating like a gale; I listen hard for the sound of lost hopes. What I hear is the traffic passing, and the blood pulsing in my ears.

There was the frightening joy of hearing the world talk to itself, and the grief of incommunicability.
JAMES AGEE
Let Us Now Praise Famous Men

OCTOBER: *Mussels*

You could wile away an afternoon on the bank of most rivers in northern Illinois without seeing very much at all happen. Whether in the country or the suburbs, or even in Chicago itself, you might see a kingfisher hustling upstream, its rattling call a seeming affront to the quiet of the early autumn day. You might see a pair of mallards foraging along the bank, paddling a little faster as they pass you by, their barely audible quacks telling of their nervousness at your presence—though if you are quiet enough, they might not even notice you. You would probably hear a squirrel rustling in the woods behind you, looking for acorns. You might see a water strider skating along the bank where the water purls behind a fallen cottonwood trunk.

Slowly, the afternoon light would shift, and some of autumn's fallen leaves would coast across the glassy surface, carried along by this slow current that wends through the woods, this muscular coil of brown water. You could spend the entire afternoon and perhaps come away with the thought that to do so was a pretty dull undertaking. Or perhaps you would say to yourself that this in fact was the essence of the natural world, that though there are undeniably dramatic events in nature—the wild thunderstorm, the periodic emergence of cicadas, a flurry of ducks along the lakeshore—these are more the exception than the rule, and what nature is about most of all is feeding and sleeping and reproducing, surviving, just getting along. What I am getting at here is that if you gave the river enough time it might instruct you about the lives of creatures that live at a pace unlike ours. It might teach you about river time, about tree time. If you sat on the bank long enough, the river might even teach you about the lives of mussels.

Northern Illinois is a good place to learn about mussels because the basin of the Mississippi River and its tributaries has long been a home for them, a place where evolution has enabled them to achieve a remarkable diversity. Here a stable climate and diverse topography enabled these mollusks to exploit an exceptional variety of ecological niches. In 1906 one Illinois Natural History Survey researcher called the upper Mississippi valley "the metropolis of the pearly freshwater mussels."

At least 299 species of mussels once lived in the United States, of which 80 have been found at one time or another in Illinois. They lived throughout the state's waterways—in lakes and ponds, in streams large and small, deep and shallow, fast-moving and gentle. Just to speak their names is to compose a sort of vernacular poetry. The rivers were once rife with the orange-foot pimpleback and the cracking pearlymussel; spike and Wabash riffleshell; tubercled blossom and Higgins eye; winged mapleleaf and round hickorynut; pondhorn, pink papershell, pyramid pigtoe, paper pondshell, and purple lilliput. One could pick out of a clear stream a plain pocketbook, fat pocketbook, or rock pocketbook, a spectaclecase, a snuffbox, a pistolgrip, a washboard. There were sheepnose, rabbitsfoot, catspaw, and monkeyface; elktoe and elephant-ear; butterfly and fawnsfoot and deertoe. There were bleufers, ring pinks, yellow sandshells, pink heelsplitters, white and purple wartybacks, and pink muckets. There were ellipses and rainbows and squawfoots and rayed beans. And we should not overlook the multifarious tiny fingernail clams: the lake, swamp, river, pond, and rhomboid; or the ridged-beak, ubiquitous, greater eastern, ornamented, perforated, Alpine, or Adam peaclams.

Now at least six of those species are extinct entirely, and at least eleven more are no longer found in Illinois. Many other species that were once widespread can now be found only in a handful of locations. Nationwide thirty-five species of mussel are extinct, and sixty-nine are on the federal endangered species list. Freshwater mussels are the most threatened family of wild animals in North America, and among the most obscure. Their plight runs throughout the braided river systems, insidious but invisible to all but the most careful observers.

The mollusks commonly known as clams (which include the freshwater mussels) are also called bivalves, for the paired half-shells—or "valves," in biological parlance—that make up the shell. The vast majority are marine creatures. Only a relative handful live in freshwater, which generally offers a less stable environment, over the long run, than the sea. The native mussels of Illinois represent three families, of which the great majority belong to the Unionidae—hence the term "unionid," which is often used in speaking about native mussels in general.

Freshwater mussels feed, like their marine cousins, by straining tiny food particles out of the water that flows past them. They are typically found with shells ajar, though the upright valves are often buried entirely in mud or sand. What biologists call the animal's anterior points down, and a muscular, fleshy protrusion known as the "foot" hangs down from that end of the shell, anchoring the animal in the silt and sand.

The posterior end is nearest the surface. Two fleshy siphons point up from it, reaching into the current. The first, the "incurrent aperture," points upstream; the animal sucks water in through it. Inside the mussel the water passes through gills that filter out tiny food particles: plankton, algae, bits of detritus. Mussels are natural water clarifiers; the water that exits through the "excurrent aperture"—the second siphon—is cleaner than what came in.

It's a simple life. The mussels live quietly, filtering out their steady diet of whatever flows by, occasionally falling prey to a raccoon or muskrat if the water is shallow enough, or a predatory fish if the mussels are young and small. If water levels drop in the heat of summer a mussel can move, slowly, by extending its foot and pulling itself along behind it, leaving a trademark trail on the riverbed. But if it doesn't need to move it won't.

Freshwater mussels are edible, but only barely so by most accounts. Certainly harvesting mussels for food has never been a major occupation on the rivers of the Midwest. Native Americans may have eaten mussel meat; no one really knows. The archeological record does tell that they must have valued the pearls freshwater mussels occasionally produce, and that they used large shells as scraping blades and smaller ones for jewelry and other ornamentation.

Pearls are formed in freshwater mussels just as they are in saltwater oysters. An irritant—often a grain of sand, but it could be any hard object—lodges between the valves, and the animal secretes paper-thin layers of mother-of-pearl around it. These layers are the same substance that makes up the shell, but they build up in concentric spheres around the object. The traditional pearl, of course, is a perfect sphere, but many natural pearls are free-form, or baroque.

American settlers didn't realize freshwater mussels could produce pearls as good as those from marine shells until 1857, when a New Jersey resident inadvertently bit one while eating a poor man's meal of boiled mussels. The jewel rush on the creek he'd been foraging in soon uncovered $115,000 worth of pearls. Fortune seekers quickly turned to other creeks and rivers, but not until 1889 did they strike pay dirt in the upper Midwest. That year pearlers found $10,000 worth of organic gems in the Pecatonica River in northern Illinois.

The rewards of pearling could be great. John Madson, in his vivid account of life on the upper Mississippi, *Up on the River*, says that one pearl found in Iowa in 1902 sold for $65,000. But the quest was always quixotic. Only a tiny fraction of harvested mussels held pearls; of those, only a tiny fraction were of high quality. Most pearlers never hit the big time.

As the pearl boom crested, though, another industry arose, one concerned not with what might lie in the mussels, but with a more certain prize: the shells themselves. In the second half of the nineteenth century buttons were commonly made by cutting thin disks from bone, antler, or marine shell, then drilling holes in them and polishing them to a high luster. It was a labor-intensive, craft-oriented business. One of its practitioners was John Boepple of Ottensen, Germany. In the 1870s he received at his workshop a box of shells collected in the Illinois River. Up till then freshwater shells had never been used much for buttons; indeed, the businessmen who operated button factories in Cincinnati and St. Paul had marine shell shipped in for raw material, little suspecting the lodes in the rivers that flowed past their very doors.

Boepple found that the Illinois shells made excellent buttons. Nevertheless, they remained a curiosity until he himself emigrated to the United States in 1887. He reached the Midwest, jobbed around, and one warm day went for a swim in the Sangamon River at Petersburg in downstate Illinois. "While in bathing one day," he later wrote, "my foot was cut, and upon examination of the cause I found the bottom of the river covered with mussel shells." Boepple resolved to take advantage of the accident. During the next three years he found rich mussel beds at several locations in Illinois and Iowa, but none better than the deposits of particularly thick shells in the Mississippi near

Muscatine, Iowa. By 1891, with the backing of investors, he had opened a small button-making factory there.

His milling technique was simple: Take a clean shell and cut round blanks out of it with a cylindrical saw blade driven by a lathe. Grind the blanks to uniform thickness on a revolving emery wheel, then drill two to four holes. A little polishing, and you had a pearly white button that might even give off a slight iridescent glimmer.

Boepple had good timing. A recent tariff on the import of marine shell had made most buttons quite expensive. The river shell, by contrast, was free to all takers. Just about anyone could harvest mussels, which belonged to no one. Within a few years Boepple had several hundred employees. By 1897 there were thirteen shell-processing plants on the Mississippi; within another year there were forty-nine, as well as twelve on other midwestern waterways. Muscatine alone boasted five button factories and twenty-eight blank-cutting works.

It was easy to collect mussels in shallow water. Many collectors used the technique Boepple had accidentally pioneered: wade barefoot until you feel shells underfoot, then gather them up in your bare hands. Others used rakes similar to those used for clamming on mudflats. But the industry's explosive growth was due at least partly to the invention of the "crowfoot bar," an ingenious device that allowed mussels to be gathered in deep water. Easy to make, it consisted of a number of short lengths of chain attached to a metal bar between four and twenty feet in length. At the end of each chain was a large multiple hook made from a number of thick strands of wire twisted together.

A collector, operating from a square-cornered, flat-bottomed wooden johnboat, had only to lower the bar to the bottom over a rich mussel bed and drift with the current for a short distance. The chains bumped along the bottom. As soon as an open mussel felt the end of a hook scrape its exposed tissue, it clamped its valves tight and held on with what literally became a death grip as it was dragged along the riverbed and, ultimately, lifted into the open air. By the time the musseler raised his bar, there might be dozens of mussels clinging to its hooks, in which case raising its weight was no mean feat. (Before long, gasoline engines were introduced to help with that chore.) A team of two men could haul up nearly a ton of mussels during a long morning's work on a productive river.

The closed mussels were ferried to shore and steamed en masse over an open fire. As they died, their muscles relaxed. The collector scraped the meat from the shells—being sure to check the soggy mass for pearls—and piled the empty valves into great heaps.

Most shells were purchased by traveling buyers, either middlemen or the agents of processing camps, who showed up at the riverside camps every couple of weeks. By 1914 high-quality shell was fetching an average of $12 to $27 a ton, though yellow sandshell—which had a large, smooth valve ideal for the carving of knife handles, hat pins, buckles, and other large novelty items—might bring several times that. Savvy harvesters increased their profits by forming cooperatives and operating their own blank-cutting machines.

In 1899 almost 24,000 tons of shell were sold in the Midwest for more than $200,000. By 1909 the average annual national harvest was around 40,000 tons. That year an estimated 2,600 mussel boats plied the Illinois River alone. The downstate town of Pearl, now an obscure little dot on the map, sported five shell-processing plants. Mussels were being harvested from eastern Ohio to eastern Oklahoma, from Louisiana to the eastern edge of the Dakotas.

Though about forty species of mussels were used in the commercial trade, only about a dozen were of real importance. Of those, a few made up the lion's share of trade, among them the yellow sandshell, the black sandshell, the pocketbook, and the mucket. The premier button mussel, however, was the ebonyshell—pearly, thick, heavy, and usually less brittle than other varieties. Its shells could almost be called meaty, and they were perfect for carving. At some sites in the upper Mississippi it grew in enormous profusion. In 1910 harvesters collected 1,600 tons of shells, 80 percent of them ebonyshells, from a few miles of rapids above Keokuk, Iowa, and sold them for $30,000.

The mussel frenzy bore all the hallmarks of the other great booms in American resources—lumber, gold, oil, pigeons, or any other natural product that was there for the taking. Transient communities sprang up overnight as collectors thronged to the richest mussel beds. They put up with horrendous living conditions. Many shellers lived in ad hoc riverside camps that, if the harvest was good, were swiftly plagued by a surfeit of mussel meat. Some was fed to pigs and chickens, some was used as fish bait, but much was either dumped back in the river or left to rot onshore. In the hot, humid valley summers the stench must have been impressive.

Out on the rivers fights broke out over access rights; one Mississippi River sheller mounted a small cannon on his johnboat—and used it. Thousands left more mundane professions for easy river pickings. When the beds at Muscatine were worked out, the collectors traveled upriver or downriver, then to the Wabash, and from there up the Illinois, and many smaller rivers. "Many of the shellers are nomadic and therefore move readily with their launches from a region of poor fishery to a better locality," wrote Robert E. Coker in a 1919 report for the U.S. Bureau of Fisheries. "It is often the case, however, that in times of low water, when the mussels are easily obtained, the farm hands, miscellaneous laborers, and others engage temporarily in shelling, using any kind of available equipment or collecting by hand. It is in such cases that good beds are often rapidly and seriously depleted."

Automation and increased efficiency swiftly swept the processing industry, with separate machines and operators responsible for cutting, grinding, drilling, polishing, and sorting. Reports were written on how to cut a maximum number of uniform blanks out of nonuniform shells. Coker was saddened that the fashion industry dictated uniformity, prizing only white buttons. "Many shells in nature have beautiful colorings of purple, salmon, or pink, but the shades are not adapted to market demands," he wrote. "It is claimed that the colors are liable to fade unevenly." By 1914 the manufacturing of buttons from freshwater shell was a $5-million-a-year industry.

The assembly-line production dramatically lowered the price

of buttons. Consumption increased commensurately. In 1891 the average American bought 37 buttons; by 1910 that figure had risen to 106.

Boepple, the founder, went bust in the boom. He was a skilled craftsman but no savvy businessman. Unable to compete with the efficient, automated plants, he became a shell consultant to the Bureau of Fisheries. In 1911 he once again cut his foot while sampling mussels in a stream; this time the cut became infected, and that winter he died of blood poisoning.

Meanwhile the mussel beds disappeared rapidly, and predictably. The first harvest took most of the enormous old shells. (In his early exploring days Boepple had found one washboard in Kentucky's Salt River that measured eight by eleven inches and, after cleaning, left a shell that weighed three and a half pounds.) The big shells were the only ones old enough to have produced large pearls, and after most of them were taken pearling pretty much died out. Next musselers collected the midsize mussels, which had the highest-quality shells (large, old shells are often eroded by years of exposure to sand and water). Then they started taking the smaller ones—and because shell was sold by weight, it took many more small ones to earn as much as had been possible with the large shells.

Once the young mussels became targets of harvesters, beds were depleted with startling rapidity. In 1912 there were only 400 boats on the Illinois, where a few years before there had been 2,600. By 1919 Coker could write, "It might be said . . . that there is no important stream in which the mussel resources now exist in anything like their former abundance."

A further blow to mussel populations came from the Army Corps of Engineers, in the form of the numerous dams thrown across the Mississippi, Illinois, and other major rivers in the first half of this century. The Illinois is a good example. The river had always had a gentle gradient, punctuated by much shallow water; during dry summers it was only marginally navigable by larger vessels. The state and the corps together built seven large dams across the river between

1919 and 1939 to maintain a consistent navigation channel at least nine feet deep and three hundred feet wide. The dams converted the free-flowing river into a series of lakes connected by short stretches of swifter water. Relatively few freshwater mussel species do well in water that isn't flowing with some velocity. The amount of suitable habitat therefore shrank precipitously, while the shallow riffles that generally supported the richest beds were wiped out almost entirely.

The effect of the dams was especially insidious when combined with wasteful modern agricultural practices. Many fields were left bare outside the growing season, subject to the worst sort of water and wind erosion. A fair amount of the state's topsoil ended up in the river, whose current was now too sluggish to carry the sediment far downstream. Instead it stayed in the big lakes and the backwater sloughs, burying mussels, aquatic plants, and other bottom fauna. The new silt bottom was far too flocculent to offer suitable footing for mussels.

Pollution, too, took its toll, especially after 1900, when engineers reversed the flow of the Chicago River, sending the great city's sewage down the Des Plaines and Illinois Rivers to the Mississippi, rather than allowing it into the lake that provided their drinking water. The change in downstream ecology was marked. In 1912 Stephen Forbes and Robert Richardson of the Illinois Natural History Survey examined the river at Morris, about sixty miles southwest of Chicago, where a fishery had flourished in the late nineteenth century. "The water here was grayish, sloppy," they wrote with admirable scientific dispassion. "The odor was continuously foul, with a distinct privy smell in the hottest weather. Bubbles of gas were continually breaking at the surface from a soft bar of sludge. . . . On the warmest days putrescent masses of soft, grayish black, mucky matter, from the diameter of a walnut to that of a milkpan, were floating on the surface."

In the early 1870s one researcher found thirty-five species of mussels in the area near Starved Rock, eighty-five miles downstream of Chicago. In 1912 Forbes and Richardson were able to find only two species there. Only half of the forty-nine species once found in the entire river survived. Even in 1966, after the adoption of modern sewage-treatment techniques, Survey malacologist (or mussel researcher) William C. Starrett was still unable to find a single living mussel upstream of Starved Rock. The same thing happened on many other streams and rivers as great diversities of species were reduced to a few, or none.

Some might blame the decline on the mussels themselves, because part of the problem lies in their intricate and still poorly understood reproductive strategy. Being more or less stationary, male and female mussels never meet. The males merely release their sperm into the river water at some time in the spring. It's not known how they know when to do this; nor is it known how a female—who is, presumably, downstream—identifies the sperm of her species when it enters her gills along with the rest of the river's organic detritus.

If all goes well, the female becomes pregnant, or "gravid." Her gills become engorged with the minuscule young, which are known as glochidia. Now comes the complicated part. The female waits until a fish approaches. Some mussels wave a fleshy appendage that looks something like a minnow and tends to attract predatory fish. When a fish comes close enough, the female shoots out a cloud of glochidia. The lucky ones end up on the fish's gills or fins, clasping on by means of tiny hooks. The flesh of the fish then builds a cyst around each one.

The glochidia—which are the size of a pinhead at most—remain on the fish typically for one to three months, feeding on fish juice. The infection is generally not significant enough to harm the host. During those months the young mussels undergo a metamorphosis, their bodies changing into adult form while barely growing in size. When the glochidia are fully adult—though still no larger than grains of sand—they drop off the fish. The current carries them, and they tumble to the riverbed. Those that land on a good substrate—ideally, a combination of mud, sand, and gravel that is neither too hard to dig into nor too soft to hold on to—bury themselves and settle down.

It's not an easy youth. The vast majority of glochidia are devoured by minnows, never find a host, latch onto a fish that gets eaten, or suffer some other fatal accident. Clearly, they must be produced in vast numbers for the species to survive. One study estimated that a single fragile papershell could produce up to 2,225,000 larvae.

To make matters more challenging, many native mussels infect only one or two species of fish. Biologists call this coevolution and don't entirely understand how it works. It's not known, for example, how the females of those species distinguish their host fish from all the nonhost species. But this elaborate reproduction is a good example of an evolutionary strategy that's very successful—until humans cause it to go awry. If mussels just released their young into the water, the young would inevitably drift downstream. It would be next to impossible for a mussel species to colonize new areas farther upstream. A fish is infinitely more mobile than a mussel. It can swim a long way in the one-to-three-month period during which a glochidium is hitching a ride. By relying on a mobile host, mussels were able to colonize not just upstream reaches of one river, but entirely new river systems.

That strategy, however, quickly proved precarious once we started messing with the rivers. A mussel that relies on a single host species can be wiped out if the host disappears. The ebonyshell, for example, once thrived throughout much of the Mississippi watershed. Its glochidia parasitized skipjack herring, fish that lived their adult lives in the ocean but came upstream as far as Minnesota to spawn. That was impressive, but it didn't help them once the Army Corps built twenty-seven dams on the big river. Today there are no ebonyshells known to live in the Mississippi north of St. Louis, site of the southernmost dam, save perhaps a few very old specimens that predate the dams. During the great summer flood of 1993, when the Corps opened the gates of its dams to allow maximum flow, some skipjacks were seen swimming upstream, where they had not been for sixty years. If some old ebonyshells survived that long, it's just possible that they could have produced a few heirs.

The most recent threat to native mussels comes from imported zebra mussels, which have spread rapidly in recent years, not only in the Great Lakes but in the upper Mississippi basin as well. They have been able to do this because their larval young—known as veligers—do not require a fish host and can thrive in a wide variety of conditions.

Zebra mussels are a saltwater species not closely related to freshwater mussels. They look innocuous—their attractive black-and-white striped valves never grow much larger than two inches in length. Like humans, they threaten other species mainly by their wild proliferation. They glue themselves en masse to hard underwater objects with a tough cement that dental researchers have eyed covetously for years. Rocks, boat hulls, water intake pipes, and native mussel shells disappear under the solid masses of black-and-white stripes. Researchers of the Illinois Natural History Survey have found snail shells encrusted with up to 190 zebra mussels on the bottom of Lake Michigan. In such cases all you can see is zebra mussels; the object they have glued themselves to disappears in their midst.

Given current rates of topsoil erosion and the resulting rates of sediment deposition in streams, it's not uncommon for native mussels (along with some beer cans and discarded tires) to be the only hard objects on the bottom of midwestern lakes and rivers. Zebra mussels attach to them like iron filings to a magnet. In covering them so thoroughly, they prevent the native mussels from taking and expelling the water necessary for feeding. Sometimes they smother the natives with their weight, or cement the valves open or closed. In addition, their feeding may clarify the water to the extent of leaving little food available for the natives.

The destruction of habitat has wiped out a few species; zebra mussels have the potential to wipe out many more. And there is little that can be done about them, short of manually scraping them from places where we don't want them—a difficult and expensive process at best. Some species that prey on zebra mussels—imported gobies and native freshwater sponges—are currently thriving in the Great Lakes, and it's likely that a natural equilibrium will take over at some point. The zebra mussel population will continue to expand explo-

sively for a while, then decline as food resources are depleted and pre-
dation and disease increase. The main question is how many native
species, their populations already strained by overharvesting, pollution, sedimentation, and other forms of habitat destruction, will be
lost in the interim.

It might be argued—and has been with growing vehemence in recent
years, as an ever-expanding population increases its demands for resources, for space—that species like native mussels *belong* on the slip-
pery slope to extinction, that it's their problem, not ours, if they can't
adapt to a changing environment: survival of the fittest. Who will
care if the mussels are gone? Not many have noticed them so far. The
great majority of those who have cared about native mussels have
been those who have wanted to make a buck off them. There are no
PBS specials about mussels, no midwestern high school football
teams named the Clams; there has never been a Society for the Protection of American Mussels or an Anti-Shelling League.

In counterargument I would point out that mussels are a superb
indicator of the health of rivers and streams. They can grow to a great
age if their habitat is in good shape. One specimen of a European
clam reportedly attained the age of 116. If these tough creatures are
dying prematurely, it's almost certain that other organisms are too.

I think there are also other reasons for worrying about mussels. I
once spent an autumn day with two malacologists who were looking
for mussels on the Kishwaukee River in northern Illinois. They spent
the day crouched over in the cold, slaty water, foraging on the bottom
like raccoons, picking up whatever shells they encountered. The mussels collected were to be relocated upstream because the area was going to be inundated with sediment by a construction project.

Late in the afternoon I looked closely at one of the mussels they
had found. It was a strange floater, or *Strophitus undulatus*, three
inches long, one and a half wide, fairly slim. Dull green algae flecked
its posterior. The rounded ends, one of the malacologists pointed
out, showed that it was a female. The valves were not fully shut. The
creamy blob of flesh that was the foot barely oozed out beyond the

shell. I could see the gills inside the body cavity—a large, formless, whitish mass. Their size, the researcher told me, indicated that the mussel was gravid.

It was strange to think of this mussel as an animal, so differently must it—she—perceive the world. She had no sensory organs I could recognize. With most animals you can sense some common ground in the eyes, a shared perception: *So you're alive too?* Not here. What could she perceive as I held her in the open air? Mussels may lead a simple life, but at that moment I knew that it was well beyond my comprehension.

My mind went over all the good, solid, practical reasons for protecting them. They are a prime indicator of environmental health. They can tell us a great deal about water pollution and the effects of agricultural runoff on river life. They serve as an index of sedimentation. Their populations reflect the well-being of the fish that serve as their hosts. They provide important services to the ecosystem, cleaning water and providing food for fish and mammals.

But looking at this individual mussel I wanted to think of her as more than a sort of living barometer. I considered whether it was possible to *feel* for the protection of mussels. When I look at a fox or squirrel or wood thrush, it isn't hard to feel a certain commonality and therefore compassion. But mussels look like glorified rocks. Indeed, if there is a basis according to which we can respect them, it must be exactly that fact. Mussels are worth protecting because they are more immobile and rooted than we can ever be, nourishing and nourished by the river to such an extent that a river without them is really no river at all. They can grow to the same age as we, accumulating a long lifetime of experience—and we have no conception, no idea at all, what their experience is like. But it's a pretty good bet that they ask no more than what the river brings, and perhaps that is the greatest lesson we can learn from them.

Narrative in the deer world is a track of scents that is passed
on from deer to deer with an art of interpretation which is
instinctive. A literature of bloodstains, a bit of piss, a whiff of
estrus, a hit of rut, a scrape on a sapling, and long gone.

GARY SNYDER
The Practice of the Wild

NOVEMBER: *Tracks*

Brushing against beggar-ticks that fastened their seeds on
my pants, I entered the November woods. Beyond the edge
the undergrowth fell away and the leaves that covered the
forest floor were the only tangible reminder of summer.
They sank brown and tan, russet and amber, into the wet-
ness of low ground that released a dank odor of decay with
my every step. Up on a slight rise they were lighter in color:
washed-out beige, or a sheen of bronze on fine red-orange.
Reddish leaves still hung like ragged flags from the limbs of

white oaks, their trunks butted with mantles of moss that glowed damp and livid green from recent rains.

Deer tracks rutted the mud along the little creek that ran from the railroad tracks toward the road and then on down the hill. Deer were so common in the area that suburban town officials talked of shooting some in order to protect the carefully landscaped shrubs and uncommon woodland wildflowers they liked to eat. In the suburbs they were protected from hunting, and from all enemies except motor vehicles; and they knew it. When I strolled along the bike trail they were reluctant to get out of the way. I felt the same impatience then as with the squirrels raiding the bird feeder. They were brazen. Their ability to live directly in our midst seemed to cheapen the experience of encountering them.

On this day, though, I wanted to see a deer. In the woods the experience meant more than it did on the trail, or on a road. In the woods the deer were like summer's green grown faded and tawny and skittish, ghosting along between the trees. They were much shier there, and consequently more interesting.

I walked slowly and carefully, treading quietly on the damp leaves, though some superstition told me that my desire itself reduced my chances. I see animals most readily when I'm not trying to do so. It's as if they know how grace grows from a lack of desire. But not thinking of deer was hard to do once I started finding more tracks. One set followed the narrow, muddy trail, thickly littered with fallen leaves, that meandered in an uneven circle inside the perimeter of the forest preserve. The other followed the creek. I followed these tracks, jumping over mud puddles, hanging onto skinny buckthorn trunks for balance. After a hundred or so yards the tracks veered from the creek in the direction of a small, dry knoll crowned with red oaks, where they vanished into the heavy leaf litter.

The forest preserve is a small rectangle about twenty miles north of the Chicago city limits, an island surrounded by roads on two sides, houses and yards on the third, the railroad on the fourth. From the roads it's a blur of trees. Only from the inside, among the trees, is it possible to see the small details—the muddy creek, the scant rises—that distinguish this place from any other. For the deer, these details define the place. The creek is a travel corridor relatively free of underbrush; the knoll is dry and grassy.

In our automotive society, we seldom take the time to perceive this sort of specific detail. We drive the roads, or perhaps are driven by them. We don't take the time to meander cross-country. Even when we walk, it is the sidewalk, the highway, the road to the train station and the mall that, far from just guiding us, define our image of the land. Across much of North America our surroundings are cut into straight-edged rectangles whose sides run dead east and west, north and south. This we take as a given. More than pollution, more than the extinction of native species and the introduction of exotics, more even than the taming of wild forest and prairie into lawn and garden, this is the primary change Western culture has wrought upon the land of North America: we have chopped it up into so many bits that it requires a great effort to think it all of a piece again. The fences run straight up the hills and across the low marshes. The lines that demarcate county, township, section, and lot show an indifference to the lay of the land that may once have seemed godlike but now, as expressed in the sweep of bland tract homes set on tiny lots where once were expansive prairies, seems arrogant, and petty. It's as if we were in such a hurry to parcel out the land that anything other than a straight line and right angle seemed a luxury. (In the Midwest, the few diagonal streets mark the approximate course of old Indian trails.) Everywhere our mark is the grid, denoted by road and fence—the parceling-out.

It is difficult to think that it has not always been this way, that in fact the land has its own logic that sometimes still defies the straight lines. You see it in the low-lying corner where the puddles always gather and freeze over, regardless what the highway department does; or in the hill of glacial steepness whose crest looks out west to where the chain of marshes once ran. You see it when the lakefront bluffs and beaches crumble and fall away during winter storms, ignorant of the breakwaters built to protect them. These features, these snapshots of processes endlessly cycling through biological and geological time, they endure, flash by them though we may.

It was to reestablish this sense of the land that I walked cross-country whenever I could while I lived in the suburbs. Even if I was going to the convenience store I might walk through the forest preserve, though at the end I would have to return to the road anyway. It was an effort. It was always quicker to take the road, and there was far less chance of getting muddy, or ending up with burrs sticking to my socks. The feeling of doing something slightly subversive helped me make the decision to go cross-country. Listening to the land, letting its contours direct the way, calls into question all our easy assumptions about our role in the world. "Every walk is a sort of crusade," wrote Thoreau, one of America's greatest walkers.

A strange thing about walking, as opposed to driving: distances often seem shorter to me when I walk. The faster we go, the more we lose the connection between places. When I drive across town, the landscape that connects starting point and destination is all exterior, a view through the window. Walk, and it becomes part of me: the fecund odor of downed leaves wet in a puddle, the tentative tapping of a downy woodpecker mining for grubs on a dead branch, the particular muddy ruts or grass-grown cracks in the sidewalk. It is the intimacy of this contact that makes the distance seem less; however many steps may make up the walk, they all start and finish on the ground.

I looked at the oaks crowning the knoll and considered how a dog, or a wolf, would be able to follow the deer trail I could not see, detecting the scent traces that clung to leaf and branch and trunk for—how long? Days and weeks, perhaps. The woods were suffused with scent trails that formed a web, as invisible to my senses, and as vital to the place's workings, as the intertwining strands of mycorrhizal fungi that tie together a forest's roots—trails that, as John Burroughs wrote, remind us of "the friction that is going on all about us, even when the wheels of life run the most smoothly. A fox cannot trip along the top of a stone wall so lightly but that he will leave enough of himself to betray his course to the hound for hours afterward." In all the world nothing is truly independent. We rub against one another, we chafe, we mingle, until we find that we are composed of trees and deer and the woods echo with our presence.

I wanted to follow those deer trails. They could help me find the deer. More important, I knew that they overlay the land in an entirely different way than did our roads. To the deer, a habitat consisting of forest preserves and private yards is all of a piece. It is all home. A fence can be leaped; plants on both sides are equally edible. I could only imagine how the deer trails flowed like clear rivulets across the land, circling and gathering the place into a perfect unity that lacked nothing. And I could only regret the extent of what remained hidden to me.

Try as I might, I couldn't find any deer that day, though I came across their tracks often enough. Once I found an area clear of leaves where a large deer—a buck, probably—had bounded along, leaving hoof imprints deep enough that the dewclaws showed clearly. I opened my notebook and drew the tracks, sketching their contours and textures in detail. This was the nearest intimacy I would feel with the deer today, I knew, this tedious procedure of translating a little bit of its trail into something I could take home. As I worked, crouched on the muddy ground, I sensed that in this act lay the beginning of literature, of history, possibly of language itself: stooping to read what the animals have been up to, and returning home and telling the story to the rest of the tribe. Learning just a little about how a wild animal lived on the land we shared, and relating the story, was the oldest thing I could ever do. Here, just for a moment, I could sense the land the old way, as it must feel to those who bound across its contours on hooves and paws.

I think it is a biological imperative that draws me out to walk, even in the cold and rain. If I work inside for two or three days and do not take a look at what's happening outside, I find myself pacing as restlessly as Rilke's panther, scarcely aware anymore of the world beyond the walls. But I can never adequately say why I need to get outside just then, and my best explanations of why I feel so much more comfortable and relaxed afterward always sound overrationalized. It's better just to walk and expect nothing; when the land flows in through my senses there hardly seems a need to explain anything.

A few days after I followed the deer trail I took a walk to the beach after a long day of desk work. It was sunset. Because the woods on the sides of the ravine were made up largely of maples whose leaves had fallen yellow, the place shone with an even, golden light that seemed to come as much from the leaf-littered ground as from above. The woods were a continuous rolling rug of glowing yellow and bronze. A sheet of leaves covered the placid creek, framing small patches of open water that still reflected luminescent sky.

Animal tracks were pressed like talismans into the hard, moist sand around the creek's outlet. The sprawling five-toe prints of raccoons mobbed the flat banks. Crows had written a neat chronology of events by dragging their middle toes over the raccoon spoor. Perpendicular to the creek danced the deeper traces of fox toes. On the hardest sand, only the sharp, parallel marks of its claws were visible. The fox had been running here, then leapt the creek, and in softer sand the impressions showed up firm and deep: four toe pads, rounded, longish, unmistakable. Here one of the middle claws had clicked on a pebble half-buried in sand and pressed it down; here the deep claw marks had filled with water.

Since the weather was cool, I knew the tracks would remain until the next storm pushed its waves over the beach, or sent its runoff coursing down the ravine, or pelted the sand with hard, cratering raindrops. In July these tracks would have dried in the sun and blown away in the wind; tracks that clearly delineate the summer night's activities at dawn can be all but indistinguishable by afternoon. These fall tracks, instead, were a modest stab at permanence.

I walked toward the path along the creek. Already the golden light was fading. Suddenly a gold-red form was coming toward me on the path. The thought registered instantly that this was a fox. In the next moment I regretted my standing on the open beach, where there was absolutely no place to hide. All I could do was stand and watch as, in a second, the fox crested a rise in the path, saw me, and turned tail. It ran back down the path, vanishing more swiftly than I could have imagined, quickly enough that I scarcely saw it at all. I cannot say, now, that I saw legs, or a tail, or eyes. I know it was a fox, but that impression was formed as much by fluid speed and shadow as by physical form. The fox left behind only the thought of sound, the barest whisper of a rustle among the leaves, a hint of passing that left me wondering whether I'd heard the trace of a footfall, or just of my desire.

The fox was gone, and yet in the gathering darkness it was as if I'd seen an apparition anyway, which, having never been fully present, could never really vanish. I walked forward to look for traces. I could see where a few leaves had been kicked up. A couple of deep scrapes in the sand at the top of the rise showed how the fox had turned around and powered off. There were no clear prints, and the signs quickly vanished along the path, where the leaf litter and the darkness both grew thicker. The trail was no more distinct than the sighting itself.

It is such moments that I commemorate when I look at tracks. The instant of seeing an animal animates the many moments spent analyzing its traces. I turned around and looked again at the prints along the creek. What, I wondered, were the raccoons snuffling after here on the beach? Did the crows fly off suddenly because a hawk swept by? Was the tail of the fox fully extended as it leapt the creek? I pictured the front legs stretched out, the claws breaking through the sand until the pads reached their perfect equilibrium, then the rebound and the next leap. The muscles compress, and stretch again. The scene slowed into a frame-by-frame mental picture, an image frozen into all the permanence a mutable mind can muster. If I looked long enough I could almost convince myself that I was there, that I saw the fox jumping the creek more clearly than the animal I really did glimpse in the shadows.

Seeing the fox was a gift. With tracking I try to make a gift of every walk. Tracking is a matter of becoming increasingly sensitive to subtlety. When I can read a story in the dirt I go home content, knowing that the deer and foxes are leading their lives undisturbed in their privacy.

They don't mind if we don't meet. And increasingly, neither do I. Just knowing they are there is often enough. The landscape we inhabit is not made solely of earth and air and plants and animals—the details are what we fill in with memory and desire, and love. Love is what does not need to be explained. Love is in the shadows, on the trail, and reading its traces is one of its own truest expressions.

The first glimpse of bird-life came just before I turned inland. The advance guard of what became a great army of gulls crossed the horizon. They were herring gulls, and in color were in keeping with the gray day. A flock of ducks flew rapidly along below the gulls and parallel to the shore line. They were moving like thought and soon left the gulls far behind. I recognized them as old squaws, wanderers from the far off Arctic. In the middle of winter the old squaw is not an uncommon bird at the southern end of Lake Michigan. When the lake is well filled with ice these northern ducks search for the stretches of open water, and there they seek rest and food. A gunner who took station at the end of the government pier in Chicago one winter's day, killed a hundred old squaws in a few hours' time. When the killing was complete, he found out that the birds were unfit for food, and the bodies of the beautiful creatures were thrown away.

EDWARD B. CLARK
Birds of Lakeside and Prairie

DECEMBER: *Ducks*

It was late October when I saw the ducks for the first time. It was shortly after the leaves had fallen, leaving the oak and maple trunks near the beach gleaming in the cold mist, crowns bare except for a scrim of ragged brown leaves that looked as though they ought to be hanging in a tobacco barn. The lake's summer luster was gone. As usual, the change had come virtually overnight, during a storm that whipped the leaves up in wet, gusting wreaths. The first big combers from the northeast wiped out the translucent blue of summer, the effervescent whitecaps, the sparkling swells, the white confetti of sails. They rolled in gray and heavy and the beach thundered under their weight. The water seemed suddenly denser, a perfect counterpart to the low, sodden sky. It was as if the lake had pulled inside itself, grown somber, as if it refused now to relinquish its hold on what little light hit its surface. Even after the storm passed it retained that dullness.

I looked through the trunks at the cool gray water and my eyes stumbled on little dark specks. It was like running a hand over a smooth board and catching a tiny splinter. The specks drew my sight out beyond the trees. They resolved themselves, barely, into ducks, floating calm and still as wooden decoys. Now they held my eyes: there, and there, and there. Hundreds of ducks. A thousand. The lake teemed: how had I missed them before?

I walked to the beach to get a better look, gripped by the notion that warm-blooded life could survive in that icy water. The flock was stretched in a long crescent that bobbed several hundred yards from shore. Through binoculars I could see they were scaups: the males plumaged in light gray and dark blue; the females dull brown, with a white band around the base of the bill that gave them a clownish look. Some preened, rubbing their backs or flanks with rounded bills, and once in a while one pattered briefly along the surface in pursuit of another. But most just floated quietly, bobbing on the swells as perfectly as liquid itself.

It was quiet at the lake, but at my back was the whole metropolis of Chicago, the city and its booming suburbs spreading out over the rich prairie loam, filling up the old cornfields and woodlots with homes and stores and offices for people, and for a moment, shivering, I thought of a line of Thoreau's: "We need to witness our own limits transgressed," he wrote, "and some life pasturing freely where we never wander." The beach was the limit. It was counterintuitive to see warm-blooded life thriving in water that would kill a person in minutes. I knew there were good solid reasons for it—insulating air spaces among the warm down feathers, a layer of subcutaneous fat, the oily water-repellent sheen that runs water off a duck's back—but on this chilly beach those were just words. As I stood there it seemed as certain as my own existence that the lake in winter was a force wholly other, a body delineated by what we are not.

The scaup raft was there often during the next month, usually stretched out in a thick line roughly parallel to the shore. Some days there might be only two hundred; a few times, I estimated, there were more than a thousand. One day I must have walked too close, because the largest flock that I saw all autumn abruptly took flight. The ducks flapped heavy-bodied across the surface, each one running away from shore and launching into the air over others still on the water. The movement started at the closer edge of the flock and flowed across it as if the whole great raft were a rug whose one edge was pulled into the air, and so the rest had to follow. It was a rare sunny afternoon, and the air grew radiant with the spray the ducks kicked up with feet and wingtips.

Their takeoff suggested panic because it was so precipitous and because waterfowl caught between air and water always seem ungainly, hung in the balance between two elements they separately master. But once in the air the flock resolved itself into exemplary order. First the ducks flew north; then those closest to me sheared off and flew south; and half of those turned again and headed north, so that there were three flocks of hundreds of ducks apiece flying one in front of the other, in opposite directions but perfect harmony. Each bird flew as smoothly and as swiftly as its neighbor, fostering a complex regularity to the way the flocks overlapped and interwove. It was an elaborate group ballet. I thought of a vast assemblage of paper cutouts pasted onto three panes of glass, and of the panes sliding effortlessly past one another, without sound, and I knew then that the flight of birds is defined as fully by the constantly changing interstices, the delicate and infinitely precise motion of air spaces, as by the solid muscles and feathers of the birds themselves.

Even when I looked through binoculars it was hard to focus on any one individual. There was no more reason to pick a given duck than any other. I looked instead at the small shards along the edges, where streaks and skeins of five and ten and fifteen ducks broke off the main masses and slivered off in odd directions. Along these edges I could identify individuals, could note which were brown females and which gray-and-blue males. But even these ducks flew in groups. When one veered, so did the others that accompanied it, shifting their course (so it seemed to me) instantaneously. How did they know when to turn? Their reflexes were probably quicker than my sight, but standing there on the beach, with the afternoon sun glinting on thousands of wings, it was hard not to think of the whole flock as a perfect sort of unity, a singleness of purpose unimaginable to our individualized human consciousness. The flock was more than the sum of its parts; it was great because it was big, because each individual duck was subsumed into a higher purpose that was exactly its own. It made me think that we cannot really know, as humans, the reliance of scaups on one another.

Once they were gone I realized how gratifying it was to see such a large flock of wild birds, though in these days of environmental doom and gloom I could hardly be gratified without wondering whether the flocks had once been much larger; without speculating that the scaups were doing so well because they were feeding on the newly abundant zebra mussels that were wreaking their own havoc in the lake, underwater, unseen; or without thinking of the flocks of other birds that were certainly, certifiably gone from the woods and fields that remained—the wild turkeys that crashed through the woods when startled into flight, the prairie chickens courting at dawn with their eerie whistlings and stampings of feet, the passenger pigeons settling into great oaks in such numbers that the branches snapped. Whenever I walked in the woods I was haunted by those birds, and by the thought of the great shoots that went on day and night, the pigeons lying dead and dying in the leaf litter in carpets so dense the easiest thing to do was to turn the hogs loose on them. I was haunted by flocks gone beyond reckoning, and so I decided to watch the ducks.

The scaups tended to stay well out on the lake—sometimes at the very limits of perception, even with binoculars—but another group of ducks, the buffleheads, often swam and fished as close to the shore as possible. They were petite birds—barely a foot long, among the smallest ducks in the world—and so seemed all the more spirited as they dove. They stayed in small flocks, the females rather drab in gray and white, the males dapper with their bright white flanks, black backs, and big white swatches across the top of their heads. Often I caught sight of them as they swam one by one from behind a break-water or pier, dark specks emerging from dark steel like corpuscles pulsing from a capillary. If I walked too close they flushed, skittering across the surface for a few seconds and then flying low over the waves, veering unexpectedly to the left and right, wingtips almost touching the swells on the downbeat, and landing another few hundred yards down the beach.

By mid-November there were ducks of one species or more on the lake nearly every day. I scanned the horizon for them with binoculars, my eyes dancing lightly across the water until they reached a dark speck, or a smudge in the sky. At that distance, my eyes were easily fooled: one day I watched a gull flying, far out, with elastic, regular wingbeats, only to have it resolve itself into a band of five or six ducks. And more than once I spotted something out of the corner of my eye—a duck diving, I thought—and watched for it to surface, but it never did; the swells just rolled onto the beach as always, implacable, revealing nothing. The lake was a trickster, throwing up shadowed riffles that looked like ducks, or rounded swells behind which the real ducks hid like entrenched soldiers.

There was a grave and fascinating desolation to the days of late fall and early winter. The sun rarely shone; when it did, it was close to the horizon, its sallow light too weak to burn away the chill that hung in the air. In the woods the wet leaves hid all traces of the wildflowers that had stood through the summer—the Solomon's-seals and tick-trefoils, asters and thoroughworts. It was as if summer had never happened. The sky was gray, the lake was gray, and the strength of its autumn waves had washed much of the sand from the beach, leaving a wilderness of rounded rock cobbles that were treacherous to walk upon. An hour's walk turned the recollection of swimming on a hot day, or lounging on soft sand, into a fantastic memory.

Like the scaups, the buffleheads were skittish in my presence. No hunting was allowed anywhere near the city; they were safe. But they must have migrated through lakes and marshes where they were hunted. They had learned to stay out of shotgun range. The arc of their migration might take them from the Yukon to the Gulf Coast. In thinking of their swift course over cold lakes and tundra ponds, cattail marshes and river sloughs, turbulent surf and quiet backwaters, it seemed to me that space and time were both compressed, for these ducks had been following the same course for thousands of years. Their claim to their icy habitat was so much older than ours, and as I watched them fly and float and preen and squabble I thought that the rising of the city along the shore where they bobbed and swam might be a matter of only passing interest to them, a brief interlude in a time scale that was almost geological in its creeping slowness.

Though my presence made them fly, the thought that these ducks had been hunted made me feel oddly more intimate with them. Not that I had any desire to shoot them down myself, or see them shot down, but somehow the knowledge that the economy of some people, somewhere, had briefly intersected with the lives and deaths of these ducks seemed a solid, physical manifestation of the allure they held for me. There are many ways to think about hunting, but on those steely late fall days, when so much life was ebbing, or hibernating, I thought of it as an active interaction with the natural world and was gripped, deep down, by the notion of seeing and feeling a duck's still-warm blood pulse and coagulate in the cold wind.

One day I walked to the beach in a drizzle and found not a single duck. I walked north and south, hoping to see one pop from behind a breakwater, or wing swiftly by, but there was nothing. Not even a gull flew. The waves broke on the beach, gentle but relentless. I walked up into the woods atop the bluff. The few brown leaves still hanging from the oaks were sodden and quiet. On the wet leaf litter I made hardly a sound. This was the full desolation of fall, I thought, when it seems as though all life has fled inward. The steel-gray lake, in its seclusion, was the perfect mirror of my own feelings. Who does not feel a little gray in fall? Is there anyone who has not experienced a slight visceral shudder when the first cold weather sweeps in, rattling the leaves, in dim memory of days when it was prudent, and necessary, to wonder whether there was enough firewood stockpiled to get through the winter; or in the much remoter memory of the times when our ancestors must have wondered whether the sun and green leaves would ever return?

One late December afternoon I went for a walk on the beach. The fog had clenched tight and now leaked a fine, cold drizzle. It was only three o'clock, but dim and gloomy already, as if the sun, even after its solstice, had continued sinking lower and lower. There had been a cold snap. A storm had heaped piles of ice on the shore and coated the grapefruit-sized cobbles with thick crystal. It was foolhardy to walk on them, but I did anyway. The lake was a solid object, dense, glassy, its swells mild. In the sheltered spaces between breakwaters ice floes jostled in the heave and fall. They were almost translucent, but around the edges, where water and friction rubbed up extra thicknesses of ice, they grew an opaque rim. The waves were muted by the ice, but once in a while one came in with enough force to break over the floes; it suddenly buried some of them, and just as quickly was sucked down again—a constant susurration of ice and water merging, separating, restless and solid both. Only a few degrees' difference between liquid and ice formed this restlessness that was at peace with itself, change that was unchanging, a constant motion that left everything in its place.

I walked north on the ice. Here and there a goldeneye or bufflehead dove into a swell. They were half obscured by fog, but once or twice I saw, or imagined that I saw, one carried upward in a wave, like a dark imperfection in translucent crystal, or a bug in amber. Otherwise it was very still. Then, after half a mile, I saw the falcon. It was a dark shape winging overhead, going south on swift, tapered wings. I raised my binoculars just in time to see the black face-mask of a peregrine. It was gone in seconds, and the overcast was still dim, but suddenly the afternoon felt a little lighter.

I walked on and soon found a dark shape, askew, where a little bare

sand remained. It was an oldsquaw, a male, dead. I was not too surprised to see him because I'd found several ducks washed up dead in
the last few weeks. Where ducks congregate in numbers, outbreaks of
botulism are not uncommon. It was probably a bad idea to touch
them. I had already found four dead oldsquaws, including one that
had been partly disemboweled by a fox or raccoon; its organs had
gleamed in the wintry air.

I used two thick sticks to pick the duck up, taking him out of the
water and onto the shelf ice. It was then that he moved, shuddering a
little as if waking up from a bad dream and pulling himself almost
erect. He raised his head. He was alive. I threw away the sticks and
picked the duck up in my hands. He was heavy and short, compactly
built, chunky. I looked in his eye, but there was none of the contact
you sometimes see there with animals. I put him down on the sand
and studied him.

He was as beautiful as an apparition conjured out of arctic mist
and salt ice. His plumage was pied: dark breast, a soft silvery white
head splotched with brown-black behind the eye, pale flanks and
neck. Long, pointed scapular feathers of delicate pearl gray lay over
his dark brown back, feathers the color of arctic light, the color of
pastel air drawn back into itself. The color of smoke. A subtle color. I
wanted to stroke those feathers, but held back. This was a duck that
had flown from the far north, that could weather the coldest tem-
peratures, that could dive at least 180 feet deep in quest of minnows,
and yet here, lying vulnerable on the sand, he seemed as fragile as the
scales on a butterfly's wing. I was afraid to touch him.

The oldsquaw's bill was short and dark but encircled with a band
of pink, and this, I think, gave the duck a friendly expression. It was
hard to know what to do: he was alive, but his expression was vacant.
If he saw me, or felt me lift him up, he gave no sign. I lifted him high
in both hands and carried him back to the water. A wall of riprap par-
alleled the beach about ten feet out holding back both slush and
waves, so at the shore the water was as smooth as a pond. I stood on a
small sandy point, reached out as far as I could, and put the duck in
the water. He sailed upright. I was glad to see that. Then a slight cur-

rent caught him—the sort of current a healthy duck would breast without effort, even a tiny bufflehead—and whirled him two yards from shore. He paddled his dark feet once, twice, and then was still. Head still erect, but showing no sign of direction or escape, he drifted.

There was nothing more to be done. The swells and ice stretched on forever into the fog; only the privacy of death was more immeasurable, a huge and silent blow that could reduce even the entire stretch of winter into a circumscribed season. I shivered a little and walked on. Over a few more breakwaters, and there I came upon the remains of a kill speckling the snow: a spray of white down, a sprinkling of bone fragments, and several small chunks of red pulp that looked like the remains of sumac berries. I could not find any large feathers. *The peregrine?* I wondered. I did not want to find anything further. I did not want to know what other feathered mortality might swoop out of the low sky. I did not want to think through what it meant to have the new year ushered in by death, however awesome its flight or beautiful its plumage. I turned back.

A herring gull was settling in where I'd left the duck. It flew off as I approached, then circled and settled onto an ice floe thirty yards beyond the riprap. The duck had washed ashore again. This time he was dead for certain. He lay on his flank, head askew. I wondered about his last act of volition. Was it those little paddles of his webbed feet? Or was there some conscious letting go, a final migration, a soaring and rush of flight that now for the first time was truly effortless, leaving only a swift and fading memory of the wind and the sound of pounding wings? Here on the icy shore it was more agreeable to think that than to look at the gull preening out there and waiting for me to go.

I pulled the body out of the water and laid it on the sandspit. I had no thought of burial because that is not the way with wild animals. Instead I patted those astonishing gray feathers that lay across the back, now fearing no damage from my uncautious touch.

It grew perceptibly darker as I knelt there. The ice that marked the way home seemed to glow brighter than the sky. I rose and walked on.

Before I had gone fifty yards the gull circled back. I climbed the highest ice mound to watch. The gull landed near the duck, walked over, prodded the body with its long yellow bill, then leaped back a little. Ever watchful, looking around, it prodded the duck again, this time barely jumping back. A third poke, and it began pulling at the duck's breast. It yanked and pulled, and each time a few downy feathers drifted onto the wet sand.

After a few minutes of this I walked back to the duck, moved as much by frustration as by curiosity. *If you just put your foot on the body*, I thought—trying to project this thought to the gull—*and pulled against it, you'd have a lot more leverage.* The gull flushed and settled back to its waiting station on the floe, having done no damage to the duck, except for a few tufts of down that rolled along the sand and drifted on the water, still fluffy, their sheen of oil intact. I realized that the gull, lacking tearing claws or beak, would not be able to open the carcass; that night a fox might come upon the body, and in the morning the gull might finish off the scraps, screaming off its competitors, who would crowd around in the air and on the ice, stealing their share. On such cold, short winter days the cycling of proteins would not take long. I walked home, glad for once to be going indoors, the exigencies of life and death as clear as I was prepared then to see them.

The white waves of the wake of
The boat that rows away into
The dawn, spread and lap on the
Sands of the shores of all the world.
KENNETH REXROTH
On Flower Wreath Hill

JANUARY: *Owls*

One night in January a screech owl entered my sleep.

I dreamt that my parents and I had to go somewhere. My father insisted on driving. In waking life it had been over six months since he'd steered the car; the last time he'd tried he'd backed into the retaining wall by the driveway. We didn't know, then, whether it was the cancer or the intended cure—the drugs and radiation—that caused his disorientation.

My mother sat in the back. The road was busy. My father

didn't seem to be driving that slowly, but traffic was constantly passing us, going fast, startling him. Finally he grew confused and pulled off into a parking lot in the forest preserve. The attendant in the ticket booth looked questioningly at us.

A large tree had been knocked over nearby. Its hollow base was exposed among a mass of roots choked with crumbling soil. I looked inside and saw a fluffy, red-brown owl looking back out at me.

I woke up scared, my breath loud in the winter-still room.

Of course they call for the same prosaic reasons as any other birds. They are finding mates; they are laying claim to territories. But the details of their family life are so dark to us, so thoroughly hidden in depths of night and in boles of old half-shattered trees, that we note only the calls, disembodied and quavering on the cold breeze.

In my family, at least, they are the only birds that ever provoked fear.

This is a matter with deep roots. In European folklore owls are bringers of bad news, often harbingers of death. The Romans, one writer claims, "were said to believe so completely in the prophecy of death brought by each owl cry that they immediately tried to capture the bird and end its life beyond all possibility of revival. Merely wringing its neck was not enough. They also burned the mangled body to a crisp and tossed the ashes into the River Tiber lest even one flake remain." The belief persisted into modern Britain, as documented by E. A. Armstrong in *The Folklore of Birds*: "W. J. Brown, writing in 1934, mentions that when he commented to an old man on the death of a mutual acquaintance he remarked: 'It weren't no more nor I expected. I come past his house one night, and there were a scret (screech) owl on his roof, scretting something horrible. I always reckon to take note of them things.'"

The birds Britons call screech owls are what we call barn owls, which with their bizarre screeching and hissing calls indeed may bring to mind lost, tormented souls. The considerably smaller species Americans know as screech owls are absent from Europe; but their whinnying calls, too, are eerie. In the New World the Mayans viewed the screech owl as a symbol of Ah Puch, a god of death; in Canada the Cree feared the closely related boreal owl, believing it could foretell the death of those who heard it call. Many cultures fear all owls, period, because of their nocturnal habits, and perhaps because their eyes glare straight ahead as ours do. I think it's this unsettling combination of familiarity and absolute foreignness that does it.

All of which frames as high drama a story my mother has told often about her father, who died before I was born. A physicist who emigrated from Germany to the United States in the 1920s, he was a rationalist who regarded religion as superstition. He worked on cosmological questions, relativity, the movement of stars, corresponded with Einstein. But he also believed, somewhat, the tales about owls.

One night not long after his retirement the family heard something fluttering in the chimney flue. No one thought much of it. The next day he worked in the garden after lunch. He came back inside and removed his shoes. My grandmother was always nagging him about walking into the house in his outdoor shoes. Then he sat down at his desk and died, just like that. A heart attack.

That evening my mother, hearing the fluttering again, opened the flue and a gray screech owl darted out, like a giant moth, and sat looking at the family from the edge of the table.

My mother isn't superstitious, but since that time she's had a thing about owls too.

Another decade later, and it was my grandmother's turn: she'd had a stroke, and spent the last eight years of her life in a nursing home. My mother drove there every few days. We children went along when we were young, and played outside on the wide lawn that grew ragged and weedy down toward the river, under great trees; or, in cold weather, we stayed indoors. What I remember most about these trips is how long they seemed; we drove a two-lane road over the river, brown and muscled in winter or wan and slow in summer drought, into the country, then a four-lane highway past fields and a farm stand.

The town was called Half Day, after the length of time a journey there from the city once required. That of course was back in horse-and-buggy days, but still our trips there felt *deep*; we drove out of the suburbs, deep into the woods by the river, then deep into the open fields beyond. Grandma was hard of hearing, confined to a wheelchair, and difficult to communicate with; we children scarcely knew what to make of her. But the trips always meant a lot to me—at least they do in memory—because they were expeditions, excursions to a place profoundly different from the surroundings around home.

About a month before my father died, at Christmastime, I took a drive past the old nursing home, which had in the meantime become a juvenile detention center. I barely recognized the place, drove past it too fast, had to circle to see it from the other side of the road. The old farm stand, miraculously, was the only place that still looked remotely familiar. All the rest was the sprawling litany of late-twentieth-century America: gleaming office complexes, cookie-cutter homes, strip malls. I rolled down my window and my breath steamed. I wondered what happens to us when we lose not only our people but even the places connected to those people. Here on the wintry road shoulder, with holiday traffic pounding by fast, I could scarcely imagine playing on the great nursing home lawn, among brightly painted Adirondack chairs. And my grandmother slipped a little farther into memory.

My owl dream came during the time of year when the weather begins to make a lot of Midwesterners a little stir-crazy—not so much because of the cold or snow or gloom, but rather because in January there's almost always a warm south wind that blows in and melts the snow and stirs us all with thoughts of spring. It's time to get outside, no matter what.

On those warm days I'd go running through the slush on the bike trail, wearing shorts though the temperature wasn't over forty, acting out a vague bodily imperative to expose my skin to the air and weather. The gusts were stiff but irregular. Patches of blue scudded across the cloudy sky; grass and bare dirt peeped from the snowbanks. There seemed a touch of exuberance in the harsh calls of crows.

Or maybe they were mocking our hopes. Maybe the crows know, as all Midwesterners eventually learn, that the January thaw is a dangerous time of year because the cold will surely return—too often in the form of particularly severe freezing or heavy snow. The thaw is a false spring. It is dangerous to transfer too much allegiance or hope to it because the body and spirit, aching for spring, are all too easily disappointed when the thermometer drops again. It would be easier to stay indoors and skip the whole affair, pretend it never happened, resign yourself to waiting until March. Or maybe April.

But winter does not brook such insouciance. Winter takes effort. Throughout the rest of the year you can glide through the seasons, hardly noticing them pass, but winter demands attention. Cars collide in slick intersections or stick in snowdrifts; trains stop when the tracks ice over, causing a sudden giddy camaraderie to break out when commuters are stranded together. Winter is a raw equation of calories burned in the furnace, in the car, in the body. Winter strips us down to the basics of food and warmth and shelter. Winter is an in-your-face season that not only inconveniences us but has the gall to remind us of our own mortality, of the retreat of life from the cold. Winter reminds us that life itself is a matter of survival whose simplest definition is not dying, not just yet.

In the winter you can feel death all around you in the brief days that are so brutally cut off by darkness; you hear it in the harsh dry rattle of trees in the cold wind and see it in the desiccated leaves whirling in the gutter before they are frozen in by sleet. We often celebrate Christmas or Chanukah facilely these days, but the ancients who established the festivals of light at the winter solstice must have recognized that these activities were a dire necessity, not a luxury; without some affirmation that light and sun and warmth would return, someday, it would be easy to slip entirely out of life when days grow short, just because the shadow worlds of night and death are so very near then.

And so one January morning, in the stillness before dawn, I didn't know what to think: was an owl foretelling a death to come, or did my own half-conscious knowledge that my father would not live long tell my dreams to call forth an owl? Either way it made me shiver, all the more so once he was taken to the hospital less than a week later, in an irreversible decline.

During that last year, while he was ill, he spent hours with the junk mail that flowed in. He returned every sweepstakes entry as if the prizes offered were a miraculous cure rather than a million dollars, a new car, a Caribbean cruise.

It's the same old American dream, isn't it, I thought: something for nothing. Fresh pigeon squabs, monster pearls, free land, the Publishers Clearinghouse—that the dollars or valuables are there for the taking if you only want them badly enough is one of our deepest national myths. Maybe the conquistadores started it with their restless craving for gold and silver and the fountain of youth. Centuries later, we still can't shake our love of the bargain. We can't resist a coupon, a fire sale, a deal, even if what we buy isn't something we need at all. Anything free becomes by definition worthwhile. We have to use it now, before it's gone, because otherwise someone else will.

No wonder we're all insecure. Like all people throughout time, we have to deal with the ordinary loss of people we love; but in addition to that we have to face the consequences of our material hunger, which is really the reflection of deep immaterial needs. The fields that twenty-five years ago could give a suburban boy a taste of an entirely different, rural landscape are gone now, sprung into more suburbs. The woods by the river have been chainsawed. The old neighborhood's changed, and no one recognizes you when you go back for a visit. No wonder the world seems to be changing so swiftly: we're losing our past.

Multiply each individual loss a thousandfold, a millionfold; add up what happens when all of us suffer the loss of old and important landscapes, and it's amazing we aren't more insecure. It's no wonder that in spite of winning the cold war, in spite of a robust economy, in spite of the fact that we live longer and have far more material wealth than any of our predecessors, we are anxious, fretful. We can't rely on any place that is significant to us remaining constant. We can't count on being able to share with our children a spot that was meaningful to us as boys or girls: it might have been bulldozed in the meantime. Indeed, that's likelier than ever, since a perfectly reasonable response to that anxiety is to compensate economically for what we're losing otherwise. Work harder. Earn more. Spend more. Money has become the great American buffer against loss. The goal is to earn enough to insulate yourself against the loss of community. Those who succeed earn the house in a gated subdivision, the Sunbelt condo, the luxury cruise. Though whether they ever escape our collective anxiety is something I doubt.

Ignore the fact that we end up paying more in the long run. Ignore the fact that when we don't know the true cost of anything we don't know its worth either. Don't count the losses. Don't look back. Buy it, use it up, desire more.

Another owl story: When he was a boy my father's family lived in subtropical South America. Small owls roosted in the attic. Every once in a while it was his job to climb upstairs and get rid of them. But they were too cute to kill, he thought, and besides, they kept the local mouse population in check. So each time he just shooed them out with a broom.

In the night they always came back.

In that place, too, the pale-skinned boy suffered the sunburns that may have led to the skin cancer that led to the lymphoma that led to the intensive-care ward. Life can appear terribly foreshortened, closing notes inherent in its opening strains, when seen from the far end.

The room was on the fifth floor of the hospital. Cold-steaming skyscrapers palisaded the pale winter horizon. It was as difficult to imagine the hot sun of South America as it was to imagine how a vigorous youth, climbing up to the attic, could possibly be transmuted into this frail body lying helpless, unconscious and withered. The glass in the window was thick, and I was glad there was no way to hear the call of any bird trembling in the cold air right outside. There were only crows and small flocks of pigeons anyway, the mundane birds of the suburbs, our daily companions.

Crows will harass owls of all species mercilessly, by the way, chasing them in flight or heckling them if perched, all the while raising a ruckus that seems almost loud enough to wake the dead.

Now my father's breathing sounded ragged and strenuous. At regular intervals the breaths grew faster, more strained. When we thought he could breathe no harder, when it seemed he must stop imminently, when it seemed he would die not from running down but rather from overheating, from working too hard, the breaths slowed down and grew quiet, so faint that now, too, it seemed he could die at any moment; but this passage from life to death would be like whispering, like a song of some bird calling far off in the woods, barely heard and then vanished and instantly doubted, the lightest giving of a final bit of air from one body into the atmosphere, which the rest of us go on breathing as long as we can.

On the last night we arranged ourselves around the bed, wife, two daughters, son, and spoke little. You could go in deep, following the waves of his breathing. You could listen until there was nothing left but the rasping rhythm of air in the dimly lit room, nothing but the essential fact of stubborn breathing, life sunk into unconsciousness but still hanging on for what seemed no good reason anymore, and then when you went out into the fluorescent hallway to go to the bathroom or stretch or get some coffee, the sight of the lights and of ordinary life going on—other visitors huddled sleeping in the lounge, the nurses chatting at the end of the hall—this sight was such a relief that it was like breaking the surface and gasping, gasping for breath after being immersed in the deep blue so long you didn't even realize anymore that you were underwater.

Maybe it is easier to die in the winter because there is less life going on all around then, less to miss. Maybe it is easier to die at night because each time we sleep it is a practice death, because then you are only slipping from one darkness into a longer one. My father, stubbornly, did not die until the morning, with the pale winter sun trying to break through clouds over the city.

He just stopped breathing. His heart kept beating, briefly, as if it could have persisted indefinitely had only the rest of the body not entered its long rebellion. No owl called. What came instead was an absence, a silence.

Outside the skyscrapers steamed in the dawn cold; pigeons dropped from roosting places under the railroad bridge and whirled over the leafless trees. As we left the hospital the day-shift doctors and nurses and patients were arriving, and they helped pull us back into the ordinary. The process of missing my father was just beginning, but already we were all pulling back a little from the brink, the void into which we had peered during the night. I thought of the time I'd been in an auto accident, how after I'd pulled to the curb, the rear bumper nearly twisted off by a drunk driver, the moment before the accident suddenly seemed a lifetime away, almost unbearably innocent, irretrievably severed from the present. When death comes it slaps you wide awake. This is extinction, life's bone-cold reminder of how irrevocably every new moment is sundered from every past we have ever known.

And so I drove my mother off toward home, through the forest preserve where a few ragged red-brown leaves still hung from the wide-crowned oaks, trembling and rustling in the wind. The streets slowly filled with weekend traffic. I was counting up my losses, and I wondered how the tendrils of this new grief would wind their way into our lives from here on out. I wondered what family next would take in the view from the fifth floor. I wondered whether they would notice the crows stealing past the window, in pairs, on wings of jet. I wondered whether they would notice that sometimes the crows look so black that it is as if a bird-shaped piece of the sky were missing, and through it you can see the lightless infinity beyond.

Confronted by the uncouth specter of old age, disease, and death, we are thrown back upon the present, on this moment, here, right now, for that is all there is.

PETER MATTHIESSEN
The Snow Leopard

FEBRUARY: *Chickadees*

This is how winter should be. This is winter according to postcard publishers: brilliant blue sky, shock-white snow crunching underfoot, a low and glancing sun that turns the gray oak trunks to gold. The air crisp. I clamber and slide my way up the hill until I reach the top of the bluff, where I stand sweating and panting a little. Beneath me the earth falls away to mounds of mingled ice and sand on the beach below.

I look out over the lake and at first see nothing but a cold desolation; a plain without features; a frightening void; the horizon a curving perfection broken at second glance by the chop of waves. The relentless churning of surf, futile and indifferent, on its rim of ice. In the depths of the ravine the air was still, but here the wind bites. It takes a bare minute before I begin to shiver.

I don't mind. I have come for precisely this. In grief there is something comforting about a place like the shore of the lake in winter. Even in sunshine it is stark, somewhat frightening, cold, unlike the bright and placid woods. Here on the bluff my body is wrenched into sympathy with my emotions. Grief is recurring gusts of wind, an endless series of jarring awakenings; you can forget for a moment what you have lost, but the memory keeps returning, over and over, though perhaps the intervals between remembering grow longer with time. And so it feels right to be cut by the cold here, to realize in the wind an intimate bodily echo of loss.

I shiver. A gull swoops by on elastic wings. Far out on the steel-gray water a raft of immaculate white ice floes drifts, moving at a rate so slow that I can barely detect it. Twigs and branches creak overhead. I stomp my boots in the snow, wiggle my toes, ball my gloved hands into fists for warmth. In a few days I will be returning to my new home in the Southwest, but for now I think about how many times I have come to this beach, in summer and in winter, as a child and as an adult, as resident and as visitor—or perhaps always as visitor, for what I seek here, I realize, is something outside myself, something beyond the human-dominated world of the city and suburbs. Something larger, and older. It is something as purely physical as the bite of the wind, as abstract as the uneasiness that comes of knowing the absolute indifference of the restless lake. It is an itch, a discomfort, and now, only a few days after the funeral, it feels much like the workings of loss.

I think of how often I have chosen to come out to the lake in cold or rainy or otherwise miserable weather, making myself uncomfortable in order to feel more alive, and it seems to me that grief functions in much the same way. It is a tragic sensation, an oceanic feeling of loss, but there is in it a kernel of celebration, a reminder of the depth of life, a reminder that life is infinitely more worth celebrating when we know it has to end someday, just as we know that the sweetness of summer and autumn are made the richer by the immovable specter of winter. If there are times when the death of my father leaves me gasping with the pain of loss, there are also times when it leaves me stunned by what feels like the icy brilliance of reality. It is an emotion not far removed from joy—joy that he lived, joy that I am living, joy that the lake wind is touching my skin, turning it pink. It feels cold and sometimes bitter but it feels. *It feels*, and that in itself is a mighty affirmation.

My eyes well with liquid; my nose is numb. As stark and joyous and tragic as the lake and its wind are, body and spirit can take it only so long. I turn and descend the bluff, crunching new steps. Within a few seconds I am out of the wind, squinting against the brightness of sun on snow. I can imagine plants rising up soon, irrepressible, out of the patches under trees that remain free of snow. Then I catch myself: it is only February; there are plenty more wintry days to come.

Suddenly, in midstep, I hear birds calling nearby: *chick-a-dee-dee!* Chickadees are common birds, permanent residents in the area. Much of the time, in years past, I'd taken them for granted because it was far more exciting to see or hear something uncommon, something more colorful than these little black-and-gray-and-white birds—a tanager, a warbler, some rare visitor. But after the chill of the lake, after the wearing emotion of the last weeks, seeing them is like being able to soften in the embrace of a close friend. I follow the sound up the ravine and soon spot the birds: five or six tiny fuzzballs energetically flitting in a thicket of saplings.

Chickadees are tiny. Indeed, much of what we see is only a downy ruff of feathers. I have held them a couple of times while helping out bird banders, and each time was astounded at the tiny, wiry frame: three-eighths of an ounce of bone and muscle and hustle bundled inside an eighth of an ounce of feathers. They can puff out those feathers to increase their insulating ability, but even so the survival of warm-blooded creatures this small in the frigid northern winter is remarkable. Chickadees manage it by building up fat reserves while foraging during the day, then burning them at night to fuel the shivering that keeps them warm.

In the Midwest, as across much of their range, black-capped chickadees are among the emblematic birds of winter. During the breeding season they are skittish, secretive; though they live throughout the suburban woodlands, they are not often seen. In the winter their behavior changes, and they come to feeders with regularity, boldly. I've stood three feet from a feeder while chickadees collected sunflower seeds; more patient bird-watchers have managed to get them to feed on their hands.

Biologists believe that chickadees and other birds grow less shy in winter merely because skittishness is physiologically expensive; calories are too precious in winter to be used on luxuries like extreme alertness and ready flight. To compensate, wintering chickadees spend most of their time in small flocks. A chickadee that roams with others has an easier time feeding itself than one that travels alone, since it can follow other flock members that have found a good food source. A flock's six or eight or ten pairs of eyes also watch for hawks or cats or owls more effectively than one pair can. That's why one can lure birds near with a screech owl call. Chickadees, nuthatches, and other small birds will flock in, scolding and harassing the apparent predator so that it cannot make a sneak attack. Many birds will do the same to a hawk. They are all potential prey, but they find safety in numbers.

Throughout the winter chickadees vocalize frequently, and it is precisely in the coldest weather that it is easiest to think of their regular *dee-dee-dee-dee* or sibilant *tseet* calls as the declaration of some exuberance, a defiant statement of survival in the face of adverse conditions: "I am here!" Ornithologists prefer to describe these notes in unemotional terms, as a purely utilitarian matter of communication and survival—chickadees, they say, call frequently so that other members of the flock know where they are without having to look.

Beginning in winter, some chickadees begin to supplement their vocabulary with a clear descending whistle: *fee-bee!* Primarily uttered by males, this song probably is territorial as the male stakes his claim to a nesting area. It is a first sign that the winter flocks are breaking up into breeding pairs. Those two breezy notes are among the best indicators that winter will not last forever. The chickadees' song, like the early swelling of willow buds, is among the greatest rewards of being a naturalist: an early indication that spring will return, even as the world remains locked in winter.

For the next half-hour I follow the chickadee flock through the bare woods, up the ravine. Finally, where the ravine turns, I hear one sing, with crystal clarity: *fee-bee!* The hairs on the back of my neck rise. It's electric. Why here? I wonder. Perhaps a good nest cavity is nearby; perhaps the trees support larger-than-usual numbers of insects here. There's nothing to show me why a chickadee would choose this spot rather than any other.

But I will take it on faith. I will believe that this is the place where through the cold and snow and bareness of winter the promise of spring wells up. I will believe that I can feel some persistence in the lives that have been lost. I will believe that they continue on through our own living minds and bodies, on and on, world without end.

There have been a few occasions in my life when, as on this afternoon, I have felt myself filled with hope for no reason save the existence of hope itself. Invisible in the distance, hidden behind the gathered leafless crowns of the oaks and maples, I hear the sharp calls of many crows spilling over the slighter chickadee sounds. They sound agitated; perhaps they are mobbing a red-tailed hawk. I think of how I would love to see a hawk, as always, practicing its ease in the air, or perched bulkily on a branch. But I decide not to track it down. I decide that this has been enough; I decide that hope can be shaped as clearly by what we do not see as by what we can. And so I turn and make my way toward home.

Source Notes

MARCH: *Geese*

The epigraph appears in Edward Abbey's essay "Lake Powell by Houseboat," part of the collection *One Life at a Time, Please* (Holt, 1987). Thoreau's chewy essay "Walking," first published in the *Atlantic Monthly* in June 1862, is more readily accessible in Thomas J. Lyons's anthology *This Incomperable Lande: A Book of American Nature Writing* (Penguin Books, 1991).

APRIL: *A Green Heron*

Thoreau's *Walden*, originally published by Ticknor and Fields in 1854, is available in a number of modern editions. The name of the bird I saw along the creek was changed in the *Check-List of North American Birds,* 6th ed., published by the American Ornithologists' Union in 1983, and changed again in "Thirty-ninth Supplement to the American Ornithologists' Union *Check-List of North American Birds,*" *The Auk* 110 (1993). The John Burroughs quote is from the essay "Sharp Eyes," in *The Writings of John Burroughs,* vol. 4 (Houghton Mifflin, 1904).

The experiment testing how well barn, long-eared, and barred owls can see is outlined in Lee R. Dice's article "Minimum Intensities of Illumination under Which Owls Can Find Dead Prey by Night," *American Naturalist* 79 (1945). The visual abilities of bald eagles and dragonflies are discussed in Edith Raskin's book *Watchers, Pursuers, and Masquerades: Animals and Their Vision* (McGraw-Hill, 1964). Werner Heisenberg is quoted in Gary Zukav, *The Dancing Wu Li Masters: An Overview of the New Physics* (William Morrow, 1979). R. H. Smythe wrote about visual efficiency, and the rods and cones of humans and raptors, in his book *Vision in the Animal World* (Macmillan, 1975). The matter of frogs and toads starving to death while surrounded by dead prey is mentioned by Katharine Tansley in *Vision in Vertebrates* (Science Paperbacks, 1965).

How evolution shaped the aesthetic intuitions of modern humans is the topic of a fascinating volume edited by Stephen R. Kellert and Edward O. Wilson, *The Biophilia Hypothesis* (Island Press, 1993). My list of Illinois's extirpated species stems from "Our Living Heritage: The Biological Resources of Illinois," edited by Lawrence M. Page and Michael R. Jeffords, *Illinois Natural History Survey Bulletin* 34 (April 1991).

MAY: *Clay*

The epigraph is drawn from the essay "The Flatness," in *A Place of Sense: Essays in Search of the Midwest,* edited by Michael Martone (University of Iowa Press, 1988). The nineteenth-century citation from the *Chicago Times* is reproduced in Michael H. Ebner's *Creating Chicago's North Shore: A Suburban History* (University of Chicago Press, 1988). For a general discussion of beachfront geology, see Wallace Kaufman and Orrin Pilkey's *The Beaches Are Moving: The Drowning of America's Shoreline* (Anchor Press/Doubleday, 1979). James Krohe Jr.'s article "On the Beach," from the Chicago *Reader,* May 22, 1987, deals with the issue of erosion control in Chicago and along the North Shore, while Harold Henderson's "Sand" in the *Reader* of October 31, 1986, addresses the lake's geology and erosion of its shore. Richard C. Berg and Charles Collinson's report "Bluff Erosion, Recession Rates, and Volumetric Losses on the Lake Michigan Shore in Illinois," *Illinois State Geological Survey Environmental Geology Notes,* no. 76 (July 1976), documents rates of beach and bluff loss along the North Shore.

JUNE: *Cicadas*

Bashō's poem appears in *On Love and Barley: Haiku of Bashō*, edited by Lucien Stryk (University of Hawaii Press, 1985). Much of my information about the natural history of cicadas, including the description of their intensity making it impossible for people to hear one another, speculation about the evolution of cicadas and their predators, computation of the productivity of cicada-hosting woodlands, and report on their taste, all come from entomologist Henry Dybas's article "It's the Year of the Cicada—In These Parts," *Field Museum Bulletin*, May 1973. A more detailed analysis can be found in M. Lloyd and H. S. Dybas, "The Periodical Cicada Problem. I. Population Ecology" and "The Periodical Cicada Problem. II. Evolution," *Evolution* 20 (1966).

The Bible quotes regarding locusts and manna are from Exodus 10:15, 16:14, and 16:31. Margaret Schevill Link's *The Pollen Path: A Collection of Navajo Myths* was published in 1956 by Stanford University Press. For information about the means by which cicadas produce sound I referred to P. T. Haskell's *Insect Sounds* (Quadrangle Books, 1961). Socrates' comment appears in Plato's *Phaedrus*, translated by Alexander Nehamas and Paul Woodruff (Hackett, 1995). Donald Culross Peattie's description of cicada singing comes from the June 8 entry in his *An Almanac for Moderns* (Putnam, 1935). For speculation about the relationship between 13- and 17-year cicadas, see, along with Lloyd and Dybas's *Evolution* articles, "1868 and All That for Magicicada," by Godfrey M. Hewitt, Richard A. Nichols, and Michael G. Ritchie, *Nature* 336 (November 17, 1988).

The wasp *Sphecius speciosus* formed the basis of Loren Eiseley's meditation on evolution and morality in the essay "The Coming of the Giant Wasps" in his book *All the Strange Hours* (Scribner, 1975).

JULY: *Edges*

Willa Cather's novel *My Ántonia* was published by Houghton Mifflin in 1918. Louis Joliet's depiction of presettlement Illinois is quoted in John Madson's *Where the Sky Began*, published by Houghton Mifflin in 1982 and reprinted by Sierra Club Books in 1985. Charles Dickens's reaction to the prairie is quoted and discussed at length in James Hurt's *Writing Illinois: The Prairie, Lincoln, and Chicago* (University of Illinois Press, 1992). Richard Manning's description of the sound of prairie sod breaking and his retelling of Walt Whitman's reaction to the prairie appear in his *Grassland: The History, Biology, Politics, and Promise of the American Prairie* (Viking Penguin, 1995).

Donald Culross Peattie's evocation of the midwestern grasslands forms the opening of his historical novel *A Prairie Grove* (Simon and Schuster, 1938).

For information about the ecology of woodland songbirds I interviewed Scott K. Robinson of the Illinois Natural History Survey, who has described his research in numerous papers. An overview, "Population Dynamics of Breeding Neotropical Migrants in a Fragmented Illinois Landscape," appears in *Ecology and Conservation of Neotropical Migrant Landbirds*, edited by John M. Hagan III and David W. Johnston (Smithsonian Institution Press, 1992).

AUGUST: *Waves*
Rachel Carson's *The Sea around Us*, published by Oxford University Press in 1951, includes a discussion of nautical terms regarding waves. For explanations of the interactions of algae, zebra mussels, and other native and non-native species I am indebted to Ellen Marsden of the Illinois Natural History Survey. The antiquity of algae is discussed in V. J. and D. J. Chapman's *The Algae* (Macmillan, 1973).

Invasive species are only one of the threats to the Great Lakes brought to light in William Ashworth's *The Late, Great Lakes: An Environmental History* (Knopf, 1986). The Great Lakes zebra mussel invasion is described in an extensive literature, including P. D. N. Hebert, C. C. Wilson, M. H. Murdoch, and R. Lazar, "Demography and Ecological Impacts of the Invading Mollusc *Dreissena polymorpha*," *Canadian Journal of Zoology* 69 (1991); and Dan Burke, "Zebras Thrive in Lake Michigan," *Lake Michigan Monitor*, holiday 1995. The threat of the species' spread into the Mississippi River system is discussed in "Floods Yield Bumper Crop of Pesky Mussels" by Laurie Goering, *Chicago Tribune*, December 8, 1993. For the interaction between nonnative goby species and zebra mussels, see "Exotic Fish Set to Battle Zebra Mussel" by Stevenson Swanson, *Chicago Tribune*, November 29, 1991; gobies and the mottled sculpin form the theme for Jerry Sullivan's "Field and Street" column in the August 11, 1995, Chicago *Reader*.

The story of the Chicago-area restoration movement is documented in William K. Stevens's *Miracle under the Oaks: The Revival of Nature in America* (Pocket Books, 1995) and currently chronicled in quarterly issues of the magazine *Chicago Wilderness*.

SEPTEMBER: *Pigeons*
The epigraph is quoted in William Hornaday's *Our Vanishing Wildlife: Its Extermination and Preservation* (Scribner, 1913). I learned about acorns and

their relationship with squirrels and other animals by reading Michael Steele and Peter Smallwood's article "What Are Squirrels Hiding?" in *Natural History* 103 (October 1994). Jacques Cartier is quoted in A. W. Schorger's comprehensive study *The Passenger Pigeon: Its Natural History and Extinction* (University of Wisconsin Press, 1955), which was also my source for some of the calculations of pigeon abundance, as well as the figures regarding prices paid for pigeons. Edward B. Clark's book *Birds of Lakeside and Prairie*, a fascinating look at the natural history of northeastern Illinois at the turn of the century, was published in Chicago by A. W. Mumford in 1901.

Alexander Wilson's observations and calculations are in Alexander Wilson and Charles Lucian Bonaparte, *American Ornithology, or the Natural History of the Birds of the United States* (Constable and Co., 1831). John James Audubon's descriptions of pigeons flying and feeding come from volume 5 of his *Birds of America,* originally published by Audubon and J. B. Chevalier from 1840 to 1844 and reprinted by Dover in 1967. Aldo Leopold's quote is in *A Sand County Almanac with Other Essays on Conservation from Round River* (Oxford University Press, 1966). A description of the 1878 nesting in Michigan can be found in an article by H. B. Roney, "Efforts to Check the Slaughter," reproduced in W. B. Mershon, *The Passenger Pigeon* (Outing, 1907).

For an illuminating discussion of the extinction of this and other species—one not entirely in agreement with my analysis—see David Quammen's rich tome *The Song of the Dodo: Island Biogeography in an Age of Extinctions* (Scribner, 1996). One source for speculation that the pigeons might return as late as the second half of the twentieth century is Henry W. Shoemaker, *The Last of the Passenger Pigeons* (Ross County [Ohio] Historical Society, 1958). The term "waste and howling wilderness" is from the poem "God's Controversy with New-England" in *The Poems of Michael Wigglesworth*, edited by Ronald A. Bosco (University Press of America, 1989).

OCTOBER: *Mussels*

James Agee's lyrical *Let Us Now Praise Famous Men* was rather obscurely published by Houghton Mifflin in 1941 and reprinted by Ballantine Books in 1966.

I am indebted to Kevin S. Cummings and Christine A. Mayer of the Illinois Natural History Survey in allowing me to share their cold, wet work and for answering my many questions about mussels. Cummings's "The Aquatic Mollusca of Illinois," *Illinois Natural History Survey Bulletin* 34 (April 1991), is a good overview of the state's bivalve families, and includes a rich lode of their names. Cummings and Mayer's *Field Guide to Freshwater Mussels of the Midwest* (Illinois Natural History Survey, 1992) will appeal to any field-guide addict.

Frank Collins Baker's comment about the "metropolis" of freshwater mussels appeared in his "A Catalogue of the Mollusca of Illinois," *Illinois State Laboratory of Natural History Bulletin* 7 (1906). John Madson wrote about the history of the freshwater pearl and shell industries in *Up on the River* (Schocken Books, 1985). Other material regarding John Boepple and the button-making industry can be found in Robert E. Coker's lengthy report "Fresh-Water Mussels and Mussel Industries of the United States," *Bulletin of the U.S. Bureau of Fisheries*, no. 36 (1921). Statistics specific to the mussel harvest and the construction of dams on the Illinois River are primarily from Laurie McCarthy Talkington, *The Illinois River: Working for Our State* (Illinois State Water Survey, 1991).

Of many sources describing the reversal of the Chicago River, one good overview is John Clayton's "How They Tinkered with a River," *Chicago History*, n.s., 1 (spring 1970). The resulting pollution of the Illinois River is described in Stephen A. Forbes and R. E. Richardson's "Studies on the Biology of the Upper Illinois River," *Illinois State Laboratory of Natural History Bulletin* 9 (1913). A comparative review of mussel abundance and extirpations can be found in William C. Starrett's "A Survey of the Mussels (Unionacea) of the Illinois River: A Polluted Stream," *Illinois Natural History Survey Bulletin* 30 (February 1971). See also "Man's Effect on the Fish and Wildlife of the Illinois River" by Harlow B. Mills, William C. Starrett, and Frank C. Bellrose, *Illinois Natural History Survey Biological Notes*, no. 57 (June 1966).

The fecundity of the fragile papershell and the longevity of the European clam are mentioned by G. Alan Solem in his book *The Shell Makers: Introducing Mollusks* (Wiley, 1974). For references regarding zebra mussels, see the August section above; mention of native sponges feeding on the invaders is made in, among other articles, "High Noon for Zebra Mussels" by Stevenson Swanson, *Chicago Tribune*, April 19, 1994.

NOVEMBER: *Tracks*

Gary Snyder's essay "Blue Mountains Constantly Walking" appears in his lovely collection *The Practice of the Wild* (North Point Press, 1990). Thoreau's quote is from "Walking." The John Burroughs quote is part of his essay "Notes by the Way," in the previously mentioned *The Writings of John Burroughs*, vol. 5.

DECEMBER: *Ducks*
Edward B. Clark's anecdote comes from his previously cited *Birds of Lakeside and Prairie*. Thoreau's quote is from the "Spring" chapter in *Walden*, also mentioned above. The figure describing how deep oldsquaws can dive, as well as much other material relating to the life history and conservation of ducks, is from Frank C. Bellrose's comprehensive *Ducks, Geese, and Swans of North America* (Wildlife Management Institute, 1976).

JANUARY: *Owls*
Kenneth Rexroth's poem sequence *On Flower Wreath Hill* is collected in his book *Flower Wreath Hill: Later Poems* (New Directions, 1991). Roman and Cree folklore, along with much other fascinating material about the cultural history of owls, appears in Virginia C. Holmgren's *Owls in Folklore and Natural History* (Capra Press, 1988). Edward A. Armstrong's classic *The Folklore of Birds* was published by Collins in 1958. The Mayan mythology of owls is described in *The Night Watchers* by Angus Cameron and Peter Parnall (Four Winds Press, 1971).

FEBRUARY: *Chickadees*
Peter Matthiessen's masterful travelogue *The Snow Leopard* was published by Viking Press in 1978. For information on the winter ecology of chickadees I found no source more useful than Susan M. Smith's *The Black-capped Chickadee: Behavioral Ecology and Natural History* (Cornell University Press, 1991).